Samuel Edward Dawson

A Study

With Critical and Explanatory Notes

Samuel Edward Dawson

A Study
With Critical and Explanatory Notes

ISBN/EAN: 9783744712378

Printed in Europe, USA, Canada, Australia, Japan

Cover: Foto ©Thomas Meinert / pixelio.de

More available books at **www.hansebooks.com**

A study

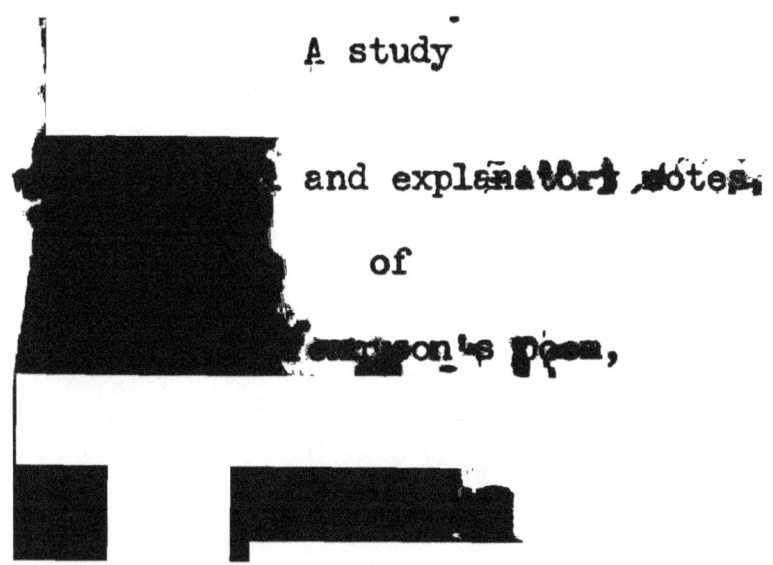 and explanatory notes,

of

Tennyson's poem,

by

Samuel Edward Dawson

TO

ALFRED TENNYSON,

𝔓𝔬𝔢𝔱 𝔏𝔞𝔲𝔯𝔢𝔞𝔱𝔢,

FIRST BARON TENNYSON D'EYNCOURT,

THIS ESSAY IS DEDICATED

IN GRATITUDE FOR THE BENEFIT DERIVED DURING
MANY HAPPY HOURS SPENT IN THE
STUDY OF HIS WORKS.

PREFACE.

It fell to the lot of the writer, as a member of a small semi-social, semi-literary society, to prepare a paper on *The Princess*, as a sequel to discussions which had previously taken place upon *The Idylls of the King* and *In Memoriam*. In studying the poem for this purpose, many passages were found in which the allusions seemed very recondite, and others in which the meaning did not lie upon the surface. Other passages were considered worthy of note on account of some peculiarity of diction or of versification. The paper as read and the notes subsequently prepared were published in the autumn of the year 1882.

The little volume attracted much more notice than was anticipated, and it soon became evident that an entire change of feeling with regard to *The*

Princess had been, for years, quietly going on. From the letters and reviews received by the writer he discovered that the epithet of "amiable enthusiast," applied to him by a courteous, though dissident, critic, was applicable to a great many people besides himself.

One letter, however, more than repaid the writer for his labour. It was from Mr. Tennyson, and, inasmuch as it contains very little personal to the essayist, and throws light upon some important literary questions regarding the manner and method of the poet's working, it seemed selfish to keep it from the large number of Tennysonians in America.

Enthusiasts in sufficient number having been found, amiable enough to buy up the first edition of this "Study," the writer, in preparing a new edition, availed himself of the opportunity to correct two errors pointed out by Mr. Tennyson. He also sought and obtained permission to publish the letter, not so much for the purpose of adding importance to his monograph, as for the deep interest with which the Laureate's own views upon the questions discussed would be received by all students of his poems

The thoughts of the great poets of former days are the heritage of every age. It is impossible to escape their influence. But, in reading for this "Study," the writer became impressed with the belief (expressed at page 2) that much injustice had been done to our present poet by strained imputations of indebtedness to his predecessors. In Virgil, Dante, Tasso, and Milton are frequent traces of their favourite authors. Such echoes of beautiful thoughts or expressions, occasionally occurring, in no degree indicate poverty of resource, but rather that wide acquaintance with literature which every educated man must possess, and that exceptional perception of the beautiful in expression which is the endowment of every poet. Many coincidences given in commentaries on Tennyson's works disappear upon verification and comparison; and such as remain are far fewer than a careful study of the works of other poets would reveal—far fewer than reviewers and commentators led the writer to expect. This question has been frequently discussed, but nowhere in so conclusive a manner as in the following letter:

Aldworth, Haslemere,
Surrey, Nov. 21st, 1882.

Dear Sir,

I thank you for your able and thoughtful essay on *The Princess*. You have seen, amongst other things, that if women ever were to play such freaks the burlesque and the tragic might go hand-in-hand.

I may tell you that the songs were not an afterthought. Before the first edition came out I deliberated with myself whether I should put songs in between the separate divisions of the poem—again, I thought, the poem will explain itself, but the public did not see that the child, as you say, was the heroine of the piece, and at last I conquered my laziness and inserted them. You would be still more certain that the child was the true heroine if, instead of the first song as it now stands,

"As thro' the land at eve we went"

I had printed the first song which I wrote,

The losing of the child.

The child is sitting on the bank of a river, and

playing with flowers—a flood comes down—a dam has been broken thro'—the child is borne down by the flood—the whole village distracted—after a time the flood has subsided—the child is thrown safe and sound again upon the bank and all the women are in raptures. I quite forget the words of the ballad but I think I may have it somewhere.

Your explanatory notes are very much to the purpose, and I do not object to your finding parallelisms. They must always recur. A man (a Chinese scholar) some time ago wrote to me saying that in an unknown, untranslated Chinese poem there were two whole lines of mine, almost word for word. Why not? are not human eyes all over the world looking at the same objects, and must there not consequently be coincidences of thought and impressions and expressions. It is scarcely possible for anyone to say or write anything in this late time of the world to which, in the rest of the literature of the world, a parallel could not somewhere be found. But when you say that this passage or that was suggested by Wordsworth or Shelley or another, I demur, and more, I wholly disagree. There was a period in my life when, as an artist, Turner for instance, takes rough sketches of landskip &c. in order to work them eventually into some great picture, so I was in the habit of chronicling, in four or five words or more, whatever might strike me as picturesque in nature. I never put these down, and many and many a line has gone away on the north wind, but some remain e. g.:

"A full sea glazed with muffled moonlight."

Suggestion:

The sea one night at Torquay, when Torquay was the most lovely sea-village in England, tho' now a smoky town. The sky was covered with thin vapour, and the moon was behind it.

" A great black cloud
Drag inward from the deep."

Suggestion:

A coming storm seen from the top of Snowdon.

In the Idylls of the King
"with all
Its stormy crests that smote against the skies."

Suggestion:

A storm which came upon us in the middle of the North Sea.

"As the water-lily starts and slides."

Suggestion:

Waterlilies in my own pond, seen on a gusty day with my own eyes. They did start and slide in the sudden puffs of wind till caught and stayed by the tether of their own stalks—quite as *true* as Wordsworth's simile and more in detail.

A wild wind shook—
    follow, follow, thou shalt win.

Suggestion:

I was walking in the New Forest. A wind did arise and—

Shake the songs the whispers and the shrieks
Of the wild wood together.

The wind, I believe, was a west-wind but, because I wished the Prince to go south, I turned the wind to the south and, naturally, the wind said "follow." I believe the resemblance which you note is just a chance one. Shelley's lines are not familiar to me, tho', of course, if they occur in the Prometheus, I must have read them.

I could multiply instances, but I will not bore you, and far indeed am I from asserting that books, as well as nature, are not, and ought not to be, suggestive to the poet. I am sure that I myself, and many others, find a peculiar charm in those passages of such great masters as Virgil or Milton where they adopt the creation of a bye-gone poet, and re-clothe it, more or less, according to their own fancy. But there is, I fear, a prosaic set growing up among us, editors of booklets, book-worms, index-hunters, or men of great memories and no imagination, who *impute themselves* to the poet, and so believe that *he*, too, has no imagination, but is for ever poking his nose between the pages of some old volume in order to see what he can appropriate. They will not allow one to say "Ring the bells," without finding that we have taken it from Sir P. Sydney—or even to use such a simple expression as the ocean "roars," without finding out the precise verse in Homer or Horace from which we have plagiarised it. (fact !)

I have known an old fish-wife, who had lost two sons at sea, clench her fist at the advancing tide on a stormy day and cry out—"Ay! roar, do! how I hates to see thee show thy white teeth!" Now if I had adopted her exclamation and put it into the mouth of some old woman in one of my poems, I daresay the critics would have thought it original enough, but would most likely have advised me to go to Nature for my old women and not to my own imagination; and indeed it is a strong figure.

Here is another little anecdote about suggestion. When I was about twenty or twenty-one I went on a tour to the Pyrenees. Lying among these mountains before a waterfall that comes down one thousand or twelve-hundred feet I sketched it (according to my custom then) in these words—

"Slow-dropping veils of thinnest lawn."

When I printed this a critic informed me that "lawn" was the material used in theatres to imitate a waterfall and graciously added "Mr. T. should not go to the boards of a theatre but to Nature herself for his suggestions."—And I *had* gone to Nature herself.

I think it is a moot point whether—if I had known how that effect was produced on the stage—I should have ventured to publish the line.

I find that I have written, quite contrary to my custom, a letter, when I had merely intended to thank you for your interesting commentary.

Thanking you again for it, I beg you to believe me

Very faithfully yours

A. TENNYSON.

P.S.—By-the-bye, you are wrong about "the tremulous isles of light": they are "isles of light," spots of sunshine coming through the leaves, and seeming to slide from one to the other, as the procession of girls "moves under *shade*."

And surely the "beard-blown" goat involves a sense of the wind blowing the beard on the height of the ruined pillar.

Mr. Ernest Myers, in *Macmillan's Magazine* for April, 1883, while reviewing "The Princess," and more particularly this "Study," has treated very happily the question of coincidences of thought and expression to be found in Tennyson's writings. His remarks upon the plan and purport of the poem are also worthy of much consideration. If, however, he would see to what extent, despite the differences

A STUDY.

Tennyson's poem of "The Princess" has been and continues to be singularly underrated. Seldom, in the universal chorus of admiration, and even adulation, which for years his work has excited, do we meet with appreciation of this his longest continuous poem. A poem, moreover, published at the age when a writer usually produces his best work—equally removed from the exuberance of youth and the chill of age, and one which has been altered and re-touched during five successive editions, until the utmost effort has been expended, and, in literary form at least, it stands out unsurpassed in perfect finish by anything in modern literature. In that respect, the "Princess" is to Tennyson's other works what the "Elegy" is to Gray's. In the adverse criticism it has called forth, we are reminded of Dr. Johnson's attack upon Milton's

"Lycidas;" indeed, both the "Princess" and "Lycidas" have continuously, and with equal justice or injustice, been reproached for the same fault, that of incongruity of plan. Both Milton and Tennyson, moreover, drew their inspiration from ancient art; but the "Lycidas" is an adaptation of Greek form and method; while the "Princess" is a transfusion of the Greek spirit into modern life. Every line of the "Lycidas" breathes of Theocritus; many are even close imitations, but while long passages of the "Princess" are pervaded by the spirit which inspired Theocritus, only in a few lines can an imitation be traced.

"Maud," like the "Princess," was received with great disappointment; but in the case of "Maud" that feeling passed away, while the "Princess" continues still to be neglected, or to be disparaged—as if it alone were unworthy of the poet's powers. Even Mr. Peter Bayne, a devotee almost of Tennyson, omits all reference to this poem in his "Lessons from my Masters." The "Idylls," "In Memoriam," "Maud," and even all the earliest poems, the "Merman" and "Oriana," receive from him, at the very least, their due meed of worship;

but the "Princess" is silently passed over, as if there, in the prime of his power, the master's skill had failed. As to adverse criticism, its nature is well shown in the following passage from the *Edinburgh Review*, written in 1855, when the poem had received its last touches:—

"The subject of the 'Princess,'" says the reviewer, "so far from being great in a poetical point of view, is partly even of transitory interest. . . . This piece, though full of meanings of abiding value, is ostensibly a brilliant serio-comic *jeu d'esprit* upon the noise about 'women's rights,' which even now ceases to make itself heard anywhere but in the refuge of exploded European absurdities beyond the Atlantic. A carefully elaborated construction, a 'wholeness,' arising out of distinct and well-contrasted parts, which is another condition of a great poem, would have been worse than thrown away on such a subject. . . . . In reading the poem, the mind is palled and wearied with wasted splendour and beauty."

It seems difficult to get further astray than this, but the last (1880) edition of Chambers's Cyclopedia of English Literature attempts it; thus:—

"The mixture of modern ideas and manners with those of the age of chivalry and romance, the attempted amalgamation of the farcical with the sentimental, renders the 'Princess' truly a 'medley,' and produces an unpleasant grotesque effect."

The result of criticism is thus summed up by Mr. Wace in the following passage of his "Study of the Life and Works of Tennyson:"—

"Although the 'Princess' was admittedly brilliant, it was thought scarcely worthy of the author. The abundant grace, descriptive beauty, and human sentiment were evident. But the medley was thought somewhat incongruous, and the main web of the tale too weak to sustain the embroidery raised upon it. D. M. Moir, the amiable 'Delta' of *Blackwood's Magazine*, says:—'Its beauties and faults are so inextricably interwoven, and the latter are so glaring and many, nay, often apparently so wilful, that as a sincere admirer of Tennyson I could almost wish the poem had remained unwritten. I admit the excellences of particular passages, but it has neither general harmony of design, nor sustained merit of execution.' A verdict more favourable, but somewhat in the same strain, may be said to be that now generally accepted."

The verdict, however, was never unanimous. There have always been a few critics with a keener sense of appreciation. A writer in the *Edinburgh Review*, in 1849, before the poem had received its present form, and consequently without the advantages of the previously quoted writer of 1855, could see unity and purpose in it. To the reviewer of 1849 the true sphere of woman's activity is not a subject to be contemptuously relegated to America; and although the lyric interludes had not at that time been inserted, he, in the following passage, instinctively touches the keynote of the poet's meaning :—

"Many passages in it have a remarkable reference to children. They sound like a perpetual child-protest against Ida's Amazonian philosophy, which, if realised, would cast the whole of the childlike element out of the female character, and, at the same time, extirpate from the soul of man those feminine qualities which the masculine nature, to be complete, must include."

The review is throughout appreciative, and is

well worth perusal even at this distance of time. Professor Hadley of Yale College,[1] one of the most elegant of American scholars, and the Rev. Charles Kingsley,[2] are among the few who resisted the general unfavourable criticism, and recognised the "Princess" as a work of art of very high order.

As we have already remarked, the poem has undergone great modifications since its first appearance in 1847. A second edition was issued in the following year, with a dedication to Henry Lushington, and very slightly retouched. In 1850 appeared the third edition, not *re-written*, as the author of "Tennysoniana" would have us think, but with very great additions, among which are the six intercalary songs. Re-writing is too strong a term for the searching revision the poem underwent in this edition, because its scope and meaning were not changed, although, by the substitution of words and other minor changes, a higher artistic polish was imparted. The artist's meaning was more fully disengaged, and the poem became sub-

---

[1] Essays, Philological and Critical, selected from the papers of James Hadley, LL.D.
[2] In *Fraser's Magazine*, reprinted in his "Miscellanies."

stantially what it is at the present time. The fourth edition was issued in 1851. In this all the passages relating to the "weird seizures" of the Prince were added; other changes were very slight. In the fifth edition, published in 1853, a passage of fifteen lines was added to the Prologue, commencing with "O miracle of women!" and with this edition the text was definitely settled. All these changes and additions, with the exception of the weird seizures of the Prince, are in reality elucidations of the initial purport of the poem. The songs and the interlude between the fourth and fifth books, like choruses in a Greek play, suggest the underlying meaning, and the concluding book, which is all new but the last thirty-eight lines, is an explanation of its form.

The great popularity of Tennyson's writings has been a puzzle to a large number of professional critics. Some have ascribed it to the supposed fact that he is the only living poet, and his success is due solely to the absence of competitors for popular favour. Frederick W. Robertson gave the true reason when he said[1] that Tennyson had

[1] Lecture II. to Mechanics' Institute at Brighton.

"vision" or "insight," and was the interpreter of his age. This idea has been pushed too far by others, who wish to discover in his poems incessant allusions to current events. A poet who suffers his thoughts to drift into the eddying currents of passing events, will soon lose his grasp upon the inner and real relations of things. He must not look too closely. In the mirror of his own poetic insight, the reflections are the permanent truths which he, like the Lady of Shalott, must weave into the magic web of his poetry, under the penalty of becoming warped and twisted by the transitory influences of his surroundings. A great poet is more than a seer of the things which are; he is a prophet of the things which are beginning to be. He is the exponent of the aspirations and the tendencies of his age. He reduces into coherent form, and clothes with beauty, the unuttered thoughts of which his age is dimly conscious. His eye is not upon the lower clouds, but, looking beyond them, he tells us which way the upper sky is passing over, for in that direction the wind will sooner or later come down. In this way poets are true seers; in advance of their age, they utter its innermost and half-conscious thought.

Now this poem, "The Princess," contains Tennyson's solution of the problem of the true position of woman in society—a profound and vital question, upon the solution of which the future of civilisation depends. But at the time of its publication, the surface thought of England was intent solely upon Irish famines, corn-laws, and free-trade. It was only after many years that it became conscious of anything being wrong in the position of women. The idea was not relegated to America, but originated there in the sweet visions of New England transcendentalists; and, long after, began in Old England to take practical shape in various ways, notably in collegiate education for females. No doubt such ideas were at the time "in the air" in England, but the dominant practical Philistinism scoffed at them as ideas "banished to America, that refuge for exploded European absurdities."

Now, however, we may say with Ida—

> The little seed they laugh'd at in the dark,
> Has risen and cleft the soil.

To these formless ideas Tennyson, in 1847, gave form, and with poetic instinct, discerning the truth, he clothed it with surpassing beauty.

He had probably long brooded over the subject. His earlier poems abound in studies of women. No other poet, save Shakespeare, has portrayed female types of such loveliness, purity, and dignity. His devotion to woman is not the lip-service of Moore and Byron, or of the amorous school of recent poetry, but it is a real service and a reverence such as that of a Galahad, moving on a far loftier plane of thought and feeling. Later, in the "Idylls of the King," he teaches us, in Guinevere, the stupendous power of woman for good or for evil. Upon her turned the success or failure of the king's noble aims, and with her fall fell the world of which the Round Table was an emblem. With such views as to the importance of woman's function in the social order, it was natural that the subject of this poem should early present itself to the poet's mind—but how to treat it? A didactic poem, an essay on woman—in the formal style of Pope's "Essay on Man"—might have suited the conventional notions of the reviewers better, but would have been foreign to Tennyson's meditative and dreamy mind. It is not his method to cut up moral reflections into two-line lengths, balance them, and drop them into the mouths of hungry votaries. Clearly with him there must be a narrative of some kind to string his pearls of thought upon; and the teaching to be Tennysonian must be in parable.

The Prologue and the Epilogue are the setting of the poem. The place—the south of England. The occasion—a festival upon the grounds of a wealthy baronet. The actors—a party of collegians on vacation, who, with a few of the well-born and cultured girls of the Hall and the neighbouring country-seats, had made a select picnic of their own in a ruined abbey. One of the collegians, a dreamy youth—the poet himself—has been rummaging in the library, and his head is full of the knightly deeds of the mediæval ancestors of the owners of the stately Hall. He joins the party, taking a volume with him, and keeping his finger in the place where is told a story of a fearless dame who defended her castle against a lawless king, and who, sallying out at the head of her retainers, utterly routed the king and his army.

O miracle of women, said the book ;
O noble heart who, being strait besieged
By this wild king to force her to his wish,
Nor bent, nor broke, nor shunned a soldier's death.

This is the key of the coming story, and this "miracle of women" is the prototype of the Princess Ida. The question at once arises—are there such women now? One of the ladies—Lilia—answers :—

There are thousands now
Such women, but convention beats them down.

Straightway, then, it is agreed that the seven youths should transfer this mediæval miracle of womanhood to modern times in a story, to which each should contribute a chapter. This is afterwards shaped and polished by the poet, who in the story assumes the character of the dreamy Prince, and pursues his lady-love through the seven cantos until she blossoms out, through the awakening power of the affections, into his ideal of perfect womanhood. Nothing can be more truthfully artistic than the gradual transition from the setting to the story itself; but just before the Poet-Prince commences, he playfully remarks upon the incongruities of a ruined abbey and a Grecian hall; a mediæval heroine, ladies' rights, and Mechanics' Institute experiments: he says—

This *were* a medley! we should have him back
Who told the "Winter's Tale" to do it for us.

This passage, and the second title of the poem, "A Medley," gave a ready-made theme for critics to dwell upon; and with wearisome iteration they dilated upon this surface-indication, without, for the most part, examining as to how far the word medley really applied. A *North British* reviewer, in 1848, wrote of "the utter want of interest, unity, and purpose" of the poem, and of "its miserable weakness and want of integrity." Others, who could not go to that length, dilated upon the improbability or impossibility of the incidents. We would not pretend to argue with any one who declared that he had no interest in any special work of art; but with what show of reason can any critic reproach "The Princess" for improbability in its incidents, and admire "The Tempest" and the

"Midsummer Night's Dream?" Who, in criticising "The Jerusalem Delivered," ever stopped to weigh probabilities about Armida's garden, or the adventures of Tancred and Clorinda? Or who ever tried to calculate the dead reckoning of Ulysses in the Odyssey? In estimating a poem the conditions assumed by the poet must be taken for granted; and we have only to inquire whether, these being assumed, the poem possesses unity, congruity, and a definite and worthy object. We have to demand also that the characters are congruous with themselves, and that the treatment of the incidents is poetical. The moment we enter the Forest of Arden in "As You Like It," we have no right to carry with us the precise rules of our work-a-day world, but we should resign ourselves to the joyous life of the inhabitants of the forest. If we find their society agreeable and improving—if their sentiments are lofty and elevating—if their language is beautiful beyond all usual speech—if their characters are consistent with themselves—and if their influence upon us is inspiriting and ennobling—let us be thankful; let us not trouble ourselves about the latitude and longitude of the abode which has charmed us, nor about the year of our Lord when it was discovered. We should apply to "The Princess" the same rules as to other similar works of imagination or fancy. To do otherwise would be as reasonable as to attempt to extract the square root of a melody, or to ascertain the cubic contents of a collection of love-songs. On close examination we shall see that the medley consists in the fact that the poem is serio-comic. The first four cantos are humorous and mock-heroic, the last three serious, touching, and almost tragic. The first four, to suit the wishes of the youths, the last three, to suit the ladies; and Lilia's song and her earnest appeal call attention to the transition.

In the first canto, the Prince is longing for the bride affianced to him in childhood. The king, his father, is raging because the Princess, disregarding the betrothal, has taken up new and strange views of the destiny of women. She has founded a university for women in one of her father's palaces, and from the wide domain around it men are ep mud upon pain of death. The king her father c'nest control her. The Prince, with two friends, (In thend Florian, steals away by night from his father's court, and starts for the southern kingdom, to appeal in person to his affianced bride, encouraged by a mysterious voice which whispers—

Follow, follow, thou shalt win.

The two fallacies which mislead the Princess are introduced here—that the woman is equal in all respects to the man, and that knowledge is all in all.

The second canto brings the three friends disguised as women into the university. That institution is humorously described, and the detection of the three friends by Florian's sister, one of the lady-lecturers, is narrated. By promising speedy departure, the young men persuade the fair professor to conceal their presence.

In the third, the mock damsels pursue their studies, and make, in the company of the Princess, an equestrian geological excursion.

The fourth canto contains the grand crash. After geologising, and astronomising, and metaphysi*sing*, the lofty lady-principal becomes hungry, *let us* like an ordinary mortal. A banquet is spread in a*long*-pavilion, and after dinner the stately P*about* calls for songs. Songs are sung by one of the ladies and by the Prince, until, in an unlucky moment, Cyril, the merriest and least sentimental of the three friends, is invited to sing some song of his northern home. He, not living in the clouds like the Prince, is much more thirsty, and has been enjoying the excellent vintage of the southern kingdom. Forgetting his disguise, and his falsetto treble, he trolls out a rollicking love-song in mellow and melodious tenor. Upon this the enraged Prince strikes him to the earth. The Princess coruscates in a burst of moral fireworks, mounts her horse, dashes off home, but, blind with rage, falls into the river and is rescued from death by the Prince.

At this point the story pauses. The ladies entreat that the mock-heroic shall cease, and Lilia claps her hands

> Like one that wishes at a dance
> To change the music.

The music is changed, and becomes serious and earnest.

In the fifth canto the Northern King has marched

B

with his army into the southern kingdom, and, anxious for the safety of his son, has surrounded the Princess Ida's domain. He has taken the king her father a prisoner. The young friends escape from the university, and reach the camp in draggled female attire. In the meantime Ida's warlike brothers have marched their troops northwards to protect their sister. The two armies face each other; but, after a parley, it is arranged that fifty knights on each side shall decide the matter in tournament—the hand of the Princess to be the reward of the Prince, if his side win. The fight takes place, the Prince is defeated, loses his bride, and is wounded nearly to death.

In the sixth canto the full strength of the poet is put forth. The field of battle, the wounded knights, the stricken Prince, the agonised father, the slowly relenting Princess, are the themes for powerful and pathetic description. Gradually the mists clear away from Ida's eyes, pity touches her heart, and all the kindly emotions crowd in fast in its train.

The seventh canto opens with one of the sweetest songs in the English language, " Ask me no more." The college is turned into an hospital; the ladies nurse the wounded knights. The transforming power of love is portrayed in these beautiful lines:—

>   Everywhere
> Low voices with the ministering hand
> Hung round the sick; the maidens came, they
>   talked,
> They sang, they read; till she not fair began
> To gather light, and she that was, became
> Her former beauty double.

But the Princess tends her lover in vain. Through long unconsciousness he passes into the delirium of fever, and her name is constantly on his lips. Finally, in the still summer night, consciousness returns, and, nearer death than life, he sees Ida at his bedside. He murmurs—

> If you be what I think you, some sweet dream,
> I would but ask you to fulfil yourself;
> But if you be that Ida whom I knew,
> I ask you nothing; only, if a dream,
> Sweet dream, be perfect. I shall die to-night,
> Stoop down, and seem to kiss me ere I die.

The whole canto must rank with the very sweetest and most finished productions of poetic art. Truth of feeling, delicacy of touch, elevation of sentiment, and absolute perfectness of diction, concur to make a climax of beauty. Then follows the epilogue or conclusion, in which, by gradual transition, the reader is brought from the fairy-land of imagination into the prosaic life of the present day without a jar or strain. He is brought back into the festival crowds at the park with which the poem commenced, and his mind is left in that state of satisfaction and quiet repose, which it is the property of every true work of art to bestow.

It will, we trust, be seen by this short sketch that the story, though it may be slight, possesses adequate motive; and proceeds with unity of conception and with gradual increase of interest, to an appropriate and satisfactory crisis and termination. In the concluding book are several passages which throw light upon the method of the poem. Ladies in the world of prosaic life dislike profoundly even the gentlest laugh at their expense. So we find the ladies in the poem, and Lilia their spokeswoman, objected to the banter in the four first cantos—

"They hated banter, wished for something real,
A gallant fight, a noble Princess—why
Not make her true heroic,—true sublime?
Or all, they said, as earnest as the close?
Which yet," replies the poet, " scarce could be."

It could not be—because the practical application of extreme theories of women's rights necessarily leads to the incongruous; and the incongruous, combined with kindly feelings, produces the humorous—in the minds of men. Women, though quicker and wittier than men, are destitute of humour. They perceive the ridiculous, but never the humorous. They never possess that outsideness of mind by which many men can contemplate their own absurdities, as it were from an outside standpoint, and enjoy them with quiet and indulgent laughter. The advocates of women's rights never seem to imagine that there is no ridicule, no feeling of superiority, in the irresistible smile which their theories provoke. They become angry, and consequently more absurd. The Prince and his two friends in draggled female attire upset the gravity of grey-bearded counsellors, and convulsed with laughter the young captains, all of whom were loyally devoted to the son of their sovereign, and whose attachment and respect were not shaken by their intense appreciation of the absurdity of the young Prince's position. In the same manner, the light-hearted Cyril shook with inward laughter at the lecture of the fair Doctor Psyche, in hood and academic gown, discoursing gravely " de omnibus rebus et quibusdam aliis," with her baby close at hand in case of need. It is not that men wish to belittle women. Cyril was at the very moment falling in love with that lactiferous Doctor of Philosophy. It is the incongruity of opposing functions which excites laughter. It has pleased the Creator to make—or, to be scientific, it has pleased the environment to evolve a being—woman, beautiful, lovable, and altogether admirable. Certain functions are given her to fulfil, towards which the same tyrannous environment has adapted every fibre of her mental and physical nature. When, turning from these, she aims to play a part to which she has not been adapted, the moment her theories are put into practice she necessarily becomes absurd; and this, combined with the attractions of her sex, excites uncontrollably the sense of humour in man. This weakness of manhood, this incapacity for seriousness, ought not to excite anger in the hearts of strong-minded ladies. Women's rights advocates insist wearisomely upon what few will dispute, that women are not inferior to men. But they go further, and demand the same education for both sexes, ignoring the difference of physique and the object of this difference, and dwelling upon the very many points in which both are alike. Now, if men were to argue from an undoubted anatomical identity,[1] and if they were to develop their neglected lacteal potentialities, and devote themselves to the alimentation of infants, would any woman be likely to fall in love with a man cultivated in that direction? Would not the blue-eyed Minerva herself burst into laughter, and would not the laughter be mixed with contempt, although, be it observed, the function in question is the most important and sacred in human society? Lilia's request, then, is easy to grant. The three following cantos are serious; and the ladies become true-heroic, because

[1] See Carpenter, "Human Physiology;" Kirke, "Physiology," for identity of structure.

they resume the position for which nature has fitted them—

And in their own clear element they move endowed with grace, beauty, and dignity.

Gentle and chivalrous though Tennyson always is, the early cantos of the poem abound with sly touches of good-natured banter, and give evidence of profound inward amusement at the weaknesses of the fair denizens of the female university. The good host who kept the inn on the confines of the sacred domain, had an awestruck reverence for his liege lady.

He always made a point to post with mares;
His daughter and his housemaid were the boys;
The land, he understood, for miles about
Was tilled by women; all the swine were sows,
And all the dogs——

On entering the gates the disguised youths find the grounds and halls full of knick-knacks and kickshaws—

Clocks and chimes, like silver hammers falling
On silver anvils.

The love of precise punctuality, so deeply implanted in the female breast, has full scope at last, as far as pretty clocks go. Everywhere are busts, and statues, and lutes, and such like *bric-à-brac* aids to knowledge—promiscuously strewed about like blue china and crockery-ware bull-dogs in a modern drawing-room. Instinctively the male reader shrinks through this part of the poem, fearful of upsetting something. Very properly also the path of knowledge, thorny to the tyrannous male, is made comfortable there. The ladies drink in science

<blockquote>Leaning deep in broidered down,</blockquote>

as is befitting. Everything matches in that university. No common pine—the professorial desk is of satin-wood. Due attention is paid to dress also; the doctors are violet-hooded, and the girls all uniformly in white—gregarious, though, even there as in the outer world. The Princess, her hair still damp after her plunge in the river, though sitting in indignant judgment upon the priests, has yet a jewel on her forehead. Then her weakness for children is apparent—a very dangerous one as we shall see.

> We like them well,——would they grew
> Like field flowers everywhere!

The difficulty of replenishing the classes seems thus early to have occurred to the Head. Difficult also is it for the august Head to overcome minor weaknesses. Thus, in the middle of a long metaphysical discussion, she makes a sudden irresistible dash to describe the prize in that subject, a golden brooch, this being dwelt on in detail; after one more digression, she comes back with great mental agility to the subject of evolution and the relativity of time. Even the solemn and sonorous despatch which she sends to her brother in the sixth canto, cannot leave her hand without the inevitable postscript. On one point, however, the Prince fairly puzzles her. He asks about the study of anatomy, which appears out of place in such an æsthetic nest. She replies—

> It pleased us not; in truth,
> We shudder but to dream our maids should a
> Those monstrous males that carve the living hound,

And cram him with the fragments of the grave.
Or, in the dark dissolving human heart,
And holy secrets of this microcosm,
Dabbling a shameless hand with shameful jest,
Encarnalise their spirits; yet we know
Knowledge is knowledge, and this matter hangs.

There is a deal of quiet humour in the reports of the lectures; the Lady Psyche's, for instance, is a model of discursiveness and condensation combined. She begins with the primal nebula, evolves the sun and planets; then the monsters, then the savage, then civilised man; glances at the Amazons, alludes to Lycia, to the Etruscans, Persians, Romans, Greeks; touches upon the customs of the Mahometans, Chinese, and Salian Franks. Then follow excursus into physiology and craniology. She compares the Hottentot, Kaffir, and Malay with Bacon, Homer, and others; brings in Sappho, Elizabeth, and Joan of Arc, and winds up in a rapture of prophecy extending to remotest ages. After this carnivale through the universe, the young men attend the classical and mathematical lectures. Then they

                              dipt in all
That treats of whatsoever is, the state,
The total chronicles of man, the mind,
The morals, something of the frame, the rock,
The star, the bird, the fish, the shell, the flower;
Electric, chemic laws, and all the rest,
And whatsoever can be taught and known.

Mark the effect upon the masculine mind—

Till, like three horses that have broken fence,
And glutted all night long breast-deep in corn,
They issued, *gorged* with knowledge.

Nothing could have saved them from an attack of mental indigestion but their female attire.

Gentle banter of this kind runs through the earlier part of the poem, with an occasional light touch only in the later books; but it does not wound, for there is no malice or depreciation in it. It is merely a surface drift; the real motive power of the poem is deeper. These songs—miracles of workmanship in which consummate art issues in perfect simplicity! They must have a he living, and an important one too, upon the theme. The young collegians, who had required that the story should be mock-heroic, felt, not only the influence of the ladies, but—

Something in the ballads which they sang,

which jarred with the burlesque. What is this something? Will it tell us of the true position and rights of women, and of the meaning of the poem? Let us take them in order, one by one. They certainly, in appearance, are foreign to the subject-matter. The first tells of a quarrel between a man and his wife, and of the reconciliation caused by the memory of their dead child—

> O there above the little grave
> We kissed again with tears.

An abiding influence, this, of the little one; reaching back from the grave.

In the next, commencing "Sweet and low," the keynote is struck in the lines—

> Rest, rest on mother's breast,
> Father will come to thee soon.

Far over the rolling waters of the western sea though the father may be compelled to wander, his thoughts are ever with his babe in the nest, his labours and privations are lightened and ennobled by worthy and unselfish purpose. Sweet influence this of the babe, reaching far across the ocean, and uniting loving hearts!

The theme of the third is a sharp antithesis, arising out of a surface analogy between the echoes of a bugle on a mountain lake, and the influences of soul upon soul through growing distances of time. In the case of the "horns of Elfland"—

> They die on yon rich sky,
> They faint on hill, or field, or river.

Fainter comes the echo in proportion to the receding distance. But how different with the influences of the soul—

> Our echoes roll from soul to soul
> And *grow* for ever and for ever.

The stress of meaning is in the word grow. The song is evidently one of married love, and the growing echoes reverberate from generation to generation, from grandparent to parent and grandchild. Once more it is unity through the family. In the first song a unity through the past, in the second a unity in the present, and in this a unity for the future. How important, then, does this relation of parentage seem to be.

The next, "Thy voice is heard through rolling drums," is a song of the influences of home and wedded love in nerving a man for the shocks and conflict of life. The face of the wife—

>   across his fancy comes,
> And gives the battle to his hands.
> A moment, while the trumpets blow,
>   He sees his brood about thy knee,
> The next, like fire he meets the foe
>   And strikes him dead—*for thine and thee.*

For thine and thee—home affection the moving spring of patriotism and heroic effort.

Such is the influence of the family—of the child, which is the bond and final cause of the family—upon man. The next song relates to their influence on women; for the life of a woman is not all sunshine, and the gift of tears is too often her only solace.

"Home they brought her warrior dead."

Leaden despair settles on the heart of the desolate

wife. The light of love is gone from her life. A maiden with the inexperience of youth lifts the face-cloth from the face of the loved one, but the fountain of tears still refuses to flow; then

> Rose a nurse of ninety years,
>   Set *his* child upon her knee,
> Like summer tempest came her tears,
>   Sweet, my child, I live for thee.

How powerfully the influence of childhood redeems from despair the desert-places of the heart, and supports the lonely mother in her sad life-work!

Finally, comes the application of these charming parables. Too much for the resolution of the Princess are these influences sweeping under the surface motives of human nature with irresistible sway. All theories are thrown aside, and in an outburst of tenderness, self-renunciation, and faith she yields in the final song—

> Ask me no more; thy fate and mine are sealed;
> I strove against the stream, and all in vain;
> Let the great river take me to the main;

> No more : dear love, for at a touch I yield ;
> Ask me no more.

Thus, in her apparent defeat does she rise to the supreme height of her womanhood.

Woman, as the complement of man, not his inferior, might exercise, and does exercise, an enormous influence upon society, independently of her influence as mother. This is one of the dominant strains of the Arthurian poems. We meet it in the "Coming of Arthur," when he is smitten by the peerless beauty of Guinevere, and dreams—

> But, were I joined with her,
> Then might we live together as one life,
> And, reigning with one will in everything,
> Have power in this dark land to lighten it,
> And power on this dead world to make it live.

The same chord is struck in the prophecy of Merlin, when in the helpless infant he discerned the glory of the blameless king, and foreshadowed also his failure; for

> could he find
> A woman in her womanhood as great

> As he was in his manhood, then, he sang,
> The twain together well might change the world.

This same strain heightens the intense pathos of the parting scene in "Guinevere." The King dwells not so much upon his own wrongs, but upon the far deeper ruin following upon the faithlessness of the Queen.

> For thou hast spoiled the purpose of my life,
> For now the whole Round Table is dissolved,
> Which was an image of the mighty world.

While this thought largely pervades the Epic of Arthur, the poem of the "Princess" has for its theme another aspect of the influence of woman upon society—her influence as mother—for she, says the Prince—

> Stays all the fair young planet in her hands.

To her, if she will take it, is committed the trust of moulding the coming generations. In her mainly is to be found the accumulated sum of the moral education painfully acquired through many generations. She is the most potent conservative force in human society. Let her refuse to play the part for which nature has designed her, and society suffers in its inmost heart. To this fundamental law all theories of blue-stockinged ladies must conform; and, therefore, our dear awesome Princess yields, through her innate goodness, to the tendency of the ages, and we kiss her feet in deep abasement that we ever could have laughed, even in our sleeves, at her vagaries.

Having thus reached the central thought of the poem, we must look for the hero or heroine of the story; that is, for the one person who comes triumphant out of the turmoil. It is not either of the kings, for they are utterly brought to nought. Nor the battered Cyril, kissing the hem of the Princess' garment for a boon; nor Arac, who has interest in nothing but the tournament. It cannot be the Prince, for he has been ignominiously thrust out of Ida's gates in draggled female clothes. Nor is it even the grand Princess, for she is vanquished at the moment of triumph. The poem is a medley in this respect, for the leading characters are all vanquished. All, save one—Psyche's baby—she is the conquering heroine of the epic. Ridiculous in the lecture-room, the babe, in the poem, as in the songs, is made the central point upon which the plot turns; for the unconscious child is the concrete embodiment of Nature herself, clearing away all merely intellectual theories by her silent influence. Ida feels the power of the child. The postscript of the despatch sent to her brother in the height of her indignation, contains, as is fitting, the kernel of the matter. She says:—

I took it for an hour in mine own bed
This morning; there the tender orphan hands
Felt at my heart, and seemed to charm from
      thence
The wrath I nursed against the world.

Rash princess! that fatal hour dashed,
      "the hopes of half the world."

Alas for these hopes! The cause, the great cause, totters to the fall when the Head confesses—

                                I felt
Thy helpless warmth about my barren breast
In the dead prime.

Whenever the plot thickens the babe appears. It is with Ida on her judgment-seat. In the topmost height of the storm the wail of the "lost lamb at her feet" reduces her eloquent anger into incoherence. She carries it when she sings her song of triumph. When she goes to tend her wounded brothers on the battle-field she carries it. Through it, and for it, Cyril pleads his successful suit, and wins it for the mother. For its sake the mother is pardoned. O fatal babe! more fatal to the hopes of woman than the doomful horse to the proud towers of Ilion—for through thee the walls of pride are breached, and all the conquering affections flock in.

We can see now that the unity, which runs through the songs, is continuous also throughout the poem; and that the songs are not snatches of melody, thrown in to diversify the interest, but are integral parts of the main motive of the piece. The true sphere of woman is in the family. The grand mission of woman is the conservation and elevation of the human race through the family. For the family is the molecule of society. It is the one and only stable and divinely appointed institution.

Other creations may fade to shapeless ruin
decaying.

Tenures of land, forms of government, creeds, thrones, republics, principalities may change and utterly decay; but, so long as this institution lasts, society can and will re-organise itself in other forms suited to the varying ages. Of this one fundamental institution, woman is the guardian. The hopes of society hang upon the hearth-altar tended by the sacred mothers of every age. It is their influence which rolls from soul to soul. They work in the coming generation, and they mould it to their will. Hence their seeming weakness; and hence also their surpassing strength and glory.

Having considered the poem with reference mainly to its unity and purpose, it remains to consider, whether each character possesses, separately, that consistency of conception which is demanded in a work of art of high order. The hard old king, rough and violent, is a type recalling the ante-historic times, when marriage was really a capture, of which the ring is a reminiscence and symbol to this day—

> Look you—Sir !
Man is the hunter; woman is his game;
The sleek and shining creatures of the chase,
We hunt them for the beauty of their skins;
They love us for it, and we ride them down.

He has a very hearty contempt for hen-pecked husbands—

> Look you ! the grey mare
Is ill to live with, when her whinny shrills
From tile to scullery, and her small goodman
Shrinks in his arm-chair; while the fires of hell
Mix with his hearth.

He is impatient with the irresolution of Ida's father—

> The spindling king;
This Gama—swamped in lazy tolerance.

And in his practical and hard-headed manner lays down the principle—

> When the man wants weight, the woman takes it up
> And topples down the scales.

The character of the Southern King is a familiar

one in every age. The bland smile, the deprecatory air, the garrulous ease, the delicate hands, indicate an ease-loving disposition, which no doubt took much quiet satisfaction when the stormy ladies departed to their college. By natural selection such a character is attracted by women of strong will, and necessarily dominated by them. He was as helpless against the two widows, who stuffed his daughter's head with theories, as he doubtless was before Ida's mother in her lifetime. His absolute powerlessness over his children, not only over Ida, but over Arac and his brothers, is manifest when the tournament is arranged in his presence in spite of his timidity. He is ignored, though shrieking

> Vainlier than a hen,
> To her false daughters in the pool, for none
> Regarded.

Upon his character the Prince meditates much—

> If this be so,
> The mother makes us most,

inclining evidently to the opinion, now generally

received, that character is inherited from the mother.

The character of Florian is drawn in a vague and colourless way. He is the companion of the Prince, his bosom friend and almost his double. "In Memoriam" was in manuscript when "the Princess" appeared, although it was not published until three years later. What Arthur Hallam was to the poet, Florian seems to be to the Prince. He calls him—

>   My other heart,
> And almost my half self; for still we moved
> Together; twinned as horse's ear and eye.

This passage suggests the parallel one in the later poem—

> But thou and I are one in kind,
>   And moulded like in nature's mint,
>   And hill, and wood, and field did print
> The same sweet forms in either mind.

Cyril's character is strongly and clearly conceived. He is the impersonation of clear, healthy, jovial common sense. No dreamer—he must be beside the Prince when the weird seizures come on; for he, better than Florian, can separate the substance from the shadow. Good at heart, though given—

> To starts and bursts
> Of revel,

practical, unspeculative, full of fun, he loves the fair young mother lecturer; and he loves her castles—

> I
> Flatter myself that always, everywhere,
> I know the substance when I see it. Well,
> Are castles shadows? Three of them? If not,
> Shall these three castles patch my tattered coat?
> For dear are these three castles to my wants,
> And dear is sister Psyche to my heart.

Not a very lofty character, but honest and genial. The wooing of the mother through the baby—

> The mother of the sweetest little maid
> That ever crowed for kisses,

betrays a sound knowledge of female nature; but then his irresistible love of fun cannot be controlled. The sight of the doctors, and the fair alumnæ, almost stifle him—

O to hear
The doctors! O to watch the thirsty plants
Imbibing.

Nothing but the dinner bell checks the current of his mirth. The stately women do not impress him. The Lady Blanche does not awe him, and he tells the Princess that—

Love and Nature, these are two more terrible

even than she. A manly and amiable character whom the fair professor will instruct in seriousness.

Naturally we think of the Lady Psyche now—a bright portrait in Tennyson's gallery of women—carefully and sympathetically drawn. We see her as the young mother, full of love for her babe, and of attachment to the Princess, taking up the nebular hypothesis in the same way as young women now, with only one child or none, three castles and too much leisure, take up willow pattern china, and ugly furniture, and dignify such pursuits with the name of culture. The loss of the babe reveals the true woman. What is court favour, or reputation, or blue china, or all the spindle-legged centipede abortions of the unlovely age of Queen Anne compared to her child :—

> Ah me, my babe, my blossom, ah my child,
> My one sweet child, whom I shall see no more!

Then follows a torrent of self-reproach—

> Ill mother that I was to leave her there,
> To lag behind, scared by the cry they made;
> The horror of the shame among them all.
> But I will go and sit beside the doors,
> And make a wild petition, night and day,
> Until they hate to hear me, like a wind
> Wailing for ever, till they open to me
> And lay my little blossom at my feet.
> My babe, my sweet Agläia, my one child.
> And I will take her up, and go my way,
> And satisfy my soul with kissing her.

Alas, dear Lady Psyche, that the mother-hunger cannot be appeased by primal nebulæ!

Conspicuous by contrast, is the Lady Blanche. She is the one thoroughly repulsive woman in all Tennyson's works. "Of faded form and haughtiest lineaments," she stands out as a type of unlovely and unloving women, self-elected champions of the cause, who are its greatest hindrances. Identifying the cause with themselves, not themselves with the cause, they fall easy victims to the hateful passions of envy and jealousy—

"The green malignant light of coming storm"

is ever in their eyes. The Lady Blanche had never felt that unselfishness with which love endows the heart, and of which a sweet reminiscence ofttimes adheres to the character, even when love has departed. Her whole soul is centred on herself; and hatred of her rival has extinguished any trace of affection which she might have had for her daughter. She pours vitriol on the memory of the husband of her youth, whom she calls a fool; but whose character, as we see it reflected in the truthful and sunny-hearted Melissa, is of a higher type than her own. Happy was he in his early escape from her awful and transcendent capacity for "nagging." Better, far better, for a man to be bewitched by the woven paces and waving hands of Vivien, or to die heart-broken by the faithlessness of Guinevere, than to live in incessant torment with a vulture ever gnawing at his heart.

The portrait of the Princess is drawn with a bold and broad touch. She is terribly in earnest. All through the poem the author has kept his finger in the old chronicle at the passage describing the "miracle of women." In the noble enthusiasm of Ida we recognise the quality which Guinevere lacked to make her the ideal wife for Arthur. Such a wife could have risen to his clear and lofty aims. She could have understood him, sympathised with him, would have clung to him, not to

Launcelot, nor another.

She could have sustained him in the loftiest stretch of his aspirations, and, if he failed, would have gone cheerfully with him to death in the ruin of his hopes. The Poet-Prince never wavers in his estimate of her—

True, she errs,
But in her own grand way; being herself
Three times more noble than three score of men.
She sees herself in every woman else,
And so she wears her error like a crown.

Like many noble women who have taken part in the women's rights movement, she thinks not of herself. The richness of the unselfishness of a loving woman has gone forth towards her own sex, with the vehement passion of a maiden for her lover. Lower and colder natures

>know not, cannot guess
>How much their welfare is a passion to us.
>If we could give them surer, quicker proof—
>Oh! if our end were less achievable
>By slow approaches, than by single act
>Of immolation; any phase of death;
>We were as prompt to spring against the pikes,
>Or down the fiery gulf, as talk of it,
>To compass our dear sisters' liberties.

This enthusiasm of unselfishness adorns all the vagaries of the Princess Ida. Her heart turns to Psyche, rather than to Blanche, because the latter has not the capacity of love even for her own child. When her ideals are shattered, and her sanctuary is invaded, she clings to Psyche's babe, and at last her devoted care of the wounded Prince gradually turned towards him her affectionate nature. The dawning of love in her heart is told with the most delicately artistic simplicity—

> Love, like an Alpine harebell hung with tears,
> By some cold morning glacier; frail at first
> And feeble, all unconscious of itself,
> But such as gathered colour day by day.

The last canto of the poem, which describes the Princess in the subdued and subduing sweetness of her womanhood, is the perfection of art and of beauty.

The Prince is, in some respects, a personation of the poet, expressing probably the poet's own views, and therefore is not drawn on a grand ideal scale. He is a foil to the Princess, necessary in order to set forth her character in its full brilliancy. Many reviewers have complained of the lack of colour in the portraiture of the Prince, with very little reason; for, to bring out the Prince more strongly, would have detracted from the unity of the poem. The Princess is not overcome by him or by his merits. She is worsted by Nature—by the constituted order of things. His character seems to have given the author more trouble than any other in the poem. It was not until after the fourth edition that he ceased to elaborate it. In that edition all the passages relating to the weird seizures of the Prince were added. These additions seem not only unnecessary and uncalled for, but are actually injurious to the unity of the work. They confuse the simple conception of his character and graft on to his personality the foreign and somewhat derogatory idea of catalepsy; for in that light does the court doctor regard them. The poet must have had some definite object in inserting them. Can it be that they are to indicate the weakness and incompleteness of the poet side of the Prince's character until he has found rest in his ideal? Then only can he say—

> My doubts are dead,
> My haunting sense of hollow shows; the change,
> This truthful change, in thee has killed it.

The dreamy Prince, haunted by doubts, and living in shadowland, by the healing influence of a happy love, wakes up to the purpose and dignity of life. Such a change is perhaps not very uncommon. Unless a man be endowed with a strong animal nature, or be dominated by some selfish passion such as ambition or avarice, life is very apt to seem purposeless and not worth the trouble of living. For such an unhealthy state of mind a worthy love is the sole remedy. Possibly some such meaning may have been in the mind of the author; but still we must resent the least imputation of catalepsy as inartistic and unnecessary.

With regard to the main theme of the poem, the Prince is in full sympathy with Ida. He aims at elevating woman, but he differs as to means. He recognises the fact that their ultimate aims must correspond with the diversity of their natures. Ida dreams of intellectual elevation only. The Prince sees clearly that moral elevation is the higher of the two; and that it is distinct and separate from knowledge. He sees that women are strong when men are weak. They, he says, are—

Not like that piebald miscellany, man;
Bursts of great heart and slips in sensual mire;
But whole and one; and, take them all in all,
Were we ourselves but half as good, as kind,
As truthful, much that Ida claims as right
Had ne'er been mooted.

The poet is evidently expressing his own views in the character of the Prince. They are, he urges—

> Truer to the law within,
> Severer in the logic of a life,
> Twice as magnetic to sweet influences
> Of earth and heaven.

When the poem was written this was strange to English ears. The Prince sees clearly what we all see now, that women lack—

> More breadth of culture;

But he is, from henceforth, enlisted with Ida.

> Henceforth thou hast a helper—me—that know
> The woman's cause is man's; they rise or sink
> Together.
> .   .   .   .   .
> If she be small, slight-natured, miserable
> How shall man grow?

Working in unison, he says—" We two "

> Will clear away the parasitic forms
> That seem to keep her up, but drag her down;

> Will leave her space to burgeon out of all
> Within her—let her make herself her own,
> To give or keep, to live and learn to be
> All that not harms distinctive womanhood.
> *For woman is not undevelopt man*
> *But diverse.*

This whole passage is very beautiful, and it is one of the cardinal passages of the poem; but it is too long to quote in full. He insists that, while gaining mental breadth, woman must not fail in childward care. This thought is the undertone of the poem. It is like the strain which runs through a grand opera. Struck in the overture it recurs again and again, and haunts us with one dominant melody. In No. 39 of "In Memoriam" the same thought occurs—

> Her office there to rear, to teach,
> Becoming, as is meet and fit,
> A link among the days, to knit
> The generations—each with each.

This is the Bugle Song in another measure. It shows us woman's mission as the preserver of the results of civilisation hardly won by the struggles of men. Upon her lips are the echoes of the ages; her true happiness is to transmit them to the coming generation. The Princess asks—

"What woman taught you this?"

To which the Prince replies, in language which appeals to the heart of every man—

                                  One
Not learned, save in gracious household ways;
Not perfect, nay, but full of tender wants;
No angel, but a dearer being, all dipt
In angel instincts, breathing Paradise,
Interpreter between the Gods and men;
Who looked all nature to her place, and yet
On tip-toe seemed to touch upon a sphere
Too gross to tread, and all male minds *perforce*
Swayed to her from their orbits as they moved
And girdled her with music. Happy he
With such a mother! faith in womankind
Beats with his blood, and trust in all things high
Comes easy to him, and, tho' he trip and fall,
He shall not blind his soul with clay.

The man who professes to distrust womankind is a traitor to the memory of his own mother and is publishing the fact that he has gone into a great deal of very bad society.

The poem of "The Princess," as a work of art, is the most complete and satisfying of all Tennyson's works. It possesses a play of fancy, of humour, of pathos, and of passion which give it variety; while the feeling of unity is unbroken throughout. It is full of passages of the rarest beauty and most exquisite workmanship. The songs it contains are unsurpassed in English literature. The diction is drawn from the treasure-house of old English poetry—from Chaucer, from Shakespeare and the poets of the Elizabethan age. The versification is remarkable for its variety; while the rhythm, in stateliness and expression, is modelled upon Milton. There are passages, which, in power over language to match sound with sense, are not excelled by anything in "Paradise Lost" for strength, or in Milton's minor poems for sweetness. The poem abounds also in evidences of the prophetic insight which has already been referred to as the mark of a true poet. In the year 1847, long before Darwin had commenced the present great revolution in scientific thought, evolutionary theories were propounded by the poet in the imaginary halls of his female university. Huxley himself could not have sketched more vividly than the Lady Psyche the progressive development of the world from the primal cosmic vapour. The Princess, with the accuracy taught only recently by the spectroscope, calls the sun "a nebulous star." When she gets her mind off the brooch, she becomes really profound in her analysis of our notions of creation as stages of successive acts. Our minds, she teaches, are so constituted that we must *of necessity* apprehend everything in the form and aspect of successive time; but, in the Almighty fiat, "*Let there be light,*" the whole of the complex potentialities of the universe were in fact hidden.

Not only is the poem satisfying in these respects. It breathes throughout that faith and hope in the future which make Tennyson the poet of a progressive age. For many excellent persons this universe is moribund. They can take pleasure in thinking that the Creator, once more foiled, is on the eve of angrily breaking up this world and beginning it all over again. Such is not the philosophy of our poet. He speaks in his own person in the epilogue. He says—

> For me the genial day—the happy crowd,
> The sport half science, fill me with a faith,
> This fine old world of ours is but a child
> Yet in the go-cart. Patience! Give it time
> To learn its limbs: *there is a hand that guides.*

This faith runs through all his works—nor is it anywhere more beautifully expressed than in his very latest volume, in the second and third stanzas of "The Children's Hospital."

Still the poem of "The Princess" is not an exhaustive solution of the question treated. All men cannot or do not marry. Millions of women pass unwedded through life. In many cases the sweetness of their nature overflows in general usefulness to others, in some cases it sours with disappointment. Millions of women have gone to dishonoured graves—" even God's providence seeming estranged"—victims to an artificial state of society.

Here are questions for more favoured ones to consider of profounder import than sun-flowers or china-pigs. Of what avail is mere knowledge before these profound social and moral problems. The ultimate outcome of all knowledge is mystery. The sources of being are hidden behind an impenetrable veil. We juggle with words and play with them as children with counters, getting out of them such meanings only as we ourselves first put in. The intellect is finite, but the affections are infinite. We know in part and we prophesy in part. Our prophecies shall fail and our knowledge vanish in a clearer dawn, but *Love*, of which woman is the priestess, abideth for ever.

NOTES.

NOTES.

―o―

PROLOGUE.

Line 63.   Or *steep-up* spout, whereon the gilded ball
   Danced like a wisp!

Steep-up as an adjective is a peculiarly Tennysonian word. It occurs again in *Queen Mary*, Act iii. Sc. 4, "the *steep-up* track of the true faith." Shakespeare, *Othello*, v. 2, has "*steep-down* gulfs of liquid fire." One is precipitously *up*, the other precipitously *down*.

Line 70.   *Dislinked* with shrieks and laughter.

Also in *Vivien*. "But she *dislinked* herself at once and rose." The use of *dis* for *un* is common in Shakespeare—discompanied for unaccompanied; discovery for uncovering; disnatured for unnatural. *Vide* Abbott's *Shakespearean Grammar*, p. 322. It occurs frequently in Tennyson.

Line 80.   *Otherwhere*,
   Pure sport.

Otherwhere has become obsolete, while *somewhere* has been retained in use. It is found in Milton's writings, but not in Shakespeare. Tennyson uses it again in *The Holy Grail*—

   And now his chair desires him in vain,
   However they may crown him *otherwhere*.

CANTO I.

Line 34. *Proxy-wedded with a bootless calf.*

This is good in poetry but bad in law, as the Princess clearly points out. The ceremony of marriage by proxy was common in the Middle Ages, but it was a fundamental principle of canon and civil law, that consent (intention) was the only basis of marriage. And here we must clear our minds of a Protestant confusion between two ceremonies, which in ante-Reformation times were distinct; viz., Espousals and Matrimony—Sponsalia et Matrimonium. The two ceremonies are thrown together in the Anglican Prayer-Book. Up to the giving away of the bride, the verbs are in the future tense; it is a promise, "I will"—that is espousals. Then the two join hands and the tense changes to the present, that is matrimony, that is the essence of the ceremony; the priest merely declares that God hath joined them, and gives the benediction of the Church. Forasmuch as they, M. and N., *have consented,* he says, *therefore* it is a marriage. The Prince and his father are clearly wrong in talking about proxy-*wedded.* It was sponsalia, espousals, not matrimonium.

There were two kinds of sponsalia and only two: Sponsalia *per verba de presente,* and sponsalia *per verba de futuro.* The first was indissoluble, because it was virtual marriage; for the parties were present giving consent. The second was not more binding than any other contract. If any condition was attempted to be attached to the first it vitiated it, and degraded it to a contract of the second class. The reason is evident. If parties to a contract *de futuro* lived together they became indissolubly married, for the consent was implied. The maxim of the civil law was—

Ubi non est consensus, non est matrimonium.

Now the Church always held (and such cases were always settled in Church courts) that espousals were not valid matrimony in the case of children espoused to each other by parents; unless both the parties consented when they grew up. After seven years there might be sponsalia, but there could not be matrimonium until the parties had arrived at years of discretion. It would be tedious to state the different opinions as to this age, certainly not before fourteen and twelve respectively.

The Princess is sound in her law. She says, Book v., that at the age of eight there could be no consent, and she had given none since. King Gama says there was a "kind of ceremony," and the Prince even does not dare, in the presence of the Princess, to call it more than a "precontract," that is *sponsalia de futuro*.

In that case the ceremony of being proxy-wedded with a bootless calf was a very bootless ceremony; and the court lawyers ought to have had their heads cut off for advising it. Because at that age the Prince and Princess were not capable of executing a procuration for that purpose.

To make this clear, let us follow the ceremony between Arthur of England and Catherine of Aragon—a wedding fraught with great events. This was an instance of espousals, *per verba de presente*, by proxy, but we must bear in mind both parties were of full age to contract *matrimonium*.

Arthur appears in person. For Catherine appears Dr. de Puebla, retinue around them suitable to the occasion. Dr. de Puebla produces a procuration from Catherine, strictly worded and limited to that one thing. People could not marry under a general power of attorney. The proxy is examined, it is signed by Catherine herself, and is in due form. Then Prince Arthur steps out and declares that he consents, then Dr. de Puebla steps forward and consents for the Princess; they join hands and accept each other. The espousals are complete and indissoluble excepting by dispensation. A few months after Catherine comes to England. She publicly ratifies the action of her attorney and receives the nuptial benediction, then goes to live with her husband; and after that the Pope himself cannot legally dissolve the marriage. The proxy in the instance in the poem was invalid, the parties not being able to give one.

NOTES.

Of course in Prince Arthur's case there was no "bootless calf." To elucidate that we must take another case. Maximilian, king of the Romans, was espoused by proxy to Anne, the heiress of Brittany, A.D. 1489. In this instance the ceremony was performed at the court of the lady; and the king's ambassador in the presence of the court put his leg, bare to the knee, into the bed of the Princess. But the Princess was a grown woman, and Maximilian had a marriageable daughter at that time betrothed to Charles VIII. of France. And it turned out that Charles VIII. broke his promise and married Anne of Brittany himself, putting double insult on Maximilian, which led to a war. This, as Hallam points out (Middle Ages, vol. i. p. 106), was a gross violation of ecclesiastical law, for the dispensation of the Pope from the first betrothal was not issued until eight days after the marriage of Anne and Charles.

This "bootless calf" ceremony, we are told by some writers, was common in England; but, as they do not quote instances, or cite canonical authorities, the statement is doubtful. An extract from Lord Bacon's *History of Henry VII.* is appended, from which it may be gathered that the ceremony was previously unknown in France. Possibly it was suggested by King Henry VII., who never allowed law to stand between him and his schemes. At that time questions of ecclesiastical law were of paramount importance in Europe. The English Reformation ostensibly originated in a dispute as to the canonical validity of the marriage of Henry VIII. with Catherine of Aragon, the widow of his deceased brother, Prince Arthur.

It must be concluded, however, that in the case of the present Princess Ida, the ceremony was very badly advised.

"The king having thus upheld the reputation of Maximilian, advised him now to press on his marriage with Britain to a conclusion, which Maximilian accordingly did; and so far forth prevailed, both with the young lady and with the principal persons about her, as the marriage was consummated by proxy, with a ceremony at that time in those parts new. For she was not only publicly contracted, but stated, as a bride, and solemnly bedded; and after she was laid, there came in Maximilian's ambassador with letters of procuration, and in the presence of sundry noble personages, men and women, put his leg stript naked to the knee, between the espousal sheets; to the end, that the ceremony might be thought to amount to a consummation and actual knowledge."—*Bacon, History of King Henry VII.*

Line 100.   A wind arose and rushed upon the South,
And shook the songs, the whispers, and the shrieks
Of the wild woods together; and a Voice
Went with it, "Follow, follow, thou shalt win."

A passage parallel to this is quoted by Mr. Wace from Shelley. It occurs in *Prometheus Unbound*, ii. 1—

> A wind arose among the pines; it shook
> The clinging music from their boughs, and then
> Low, sweet, faint sounds, like the farewell of ghosts,
> Were heard; "Oh follow, follow, follow me!"

and must have, consciously or unconsciously, dwelt in Tennyson's memory when writing these lines.

Line 110.   And so by *tilth* and *grange*.

In this sense, of land which is being tilled, the word is rare. It is found in Milton, *Par. Lost*, xi. 430—

> Beheld a field,
> Part arable and *tilth*, whereon were sheaves
> New reaped.

E

In *Enoch Arden*, 676, it is used again—

> Or withered holt, or *tilth* or pasturage.

Grange—originally the barn or building in which grain was stored ; now applied to any group of farm buildings

Line 111.   And *blowing bosks* of wilderness.

Uncultivated thickets blooming with wild flowers. Milton has "*blowing* banks." *Bosk* is an abbreviation of *boscage*, an old French word (now *bois*). This latter word is a favourite with Tennyson, *e.g.*, *Dream of Fair Women*, 51—

> Thridding the sombre *boscage* of the wood.

And again, in his last volume, in *Sir John Oldcastle*—

> Rather to thee, green *boscage*—work of God.

Shakespeare's *Tempest*, iv. 1, has—

> My *bosky* acres and my unshrubbed down.

A passage precisely parallel occurs in *Boadicea*—

> Fear not, isle of *blowing woodland*, isle of silvery parapets!"

Line 115.   But bland the smile that, like a wrinkling wind
On glassy water, drove his cheek in lines.

These lines are not in the first or second editions. The third edition reads—

> But bland the smile *that puckered up his cheeks.*

Mr. Wace quotes the following parallel passage from Shelley—*Prince Athanase*, part ii.—

>   O'er the vision wan
> Of Athanase, a ruffling atmosphere
> Of dark emotion, *a swift shadow* ran
> Like wind upon some forest-bosomed lake
> *Glassy* and dark.

Line 135.   Knowledge, so my daughter held, Was all in all.

This is the central point of the Princess' delusion. Some have thought that Tennyson borrowed the idea of his Poem from Johnson's *Rasselas*. It is a long way from *Rasselas* to *The Princess*. The following is the only passage upon which this theory is based—a very slender support :—

"The princess thought, that of all sublunary things, knowledge was the best : she desired, first, to learn all sciences, and then proposed to found a college of learned women, in which she would preside, that, by conversing with the old, and educating the young, she might divide her time between the acquisition and communication of wisdom, and raise up for the next age models of prudence and patterns of piety."—*Rasselas*.

Others suppose that the idea was suggested by *Love's Labour's Lost*, i. 1—

>   Our court shall be a little Academe,
> Still and contemplative in living art.

This is far more probable, because the plot of that play turns on the attempted seclusion of a king and his attendants for three years in study, during which time no woman was to approach the court. The disturbing influence of love upon such a plan is the motive of the comedy. This theory is perhaps hinted at in the lines in the Prologue—

>   We should have him back
> Who told the "Winter's Tale" to do it for us.

Line 204.   Him we gave a costly bribe
        To *guerdon* silence.

Rare as a transitive verb, but so used by Chaucer, *e.g.*, *Court of Love*, iv. 30—
        But guerdon me liche as I may deserve.

And by Shakespeare, 2 *Hen. VI.*, i. 4—
        See you well guerdoned for these good deserts.

And again by Tennyson in *Love thou thy land*—
        It grows to guerdon afterdays.

This word *guerdon* has a curious history. It originated in the old High German *widarlôn*, "recompense," and was corrupted, by the aid of the Latin *donum*, into Low Latin *widerdonum*, a half Latin, half Teutonic compound. By the usual change of *w* into *gui* this was changed into the Romance verb *guidardonare*. Thence the Italian noun *guiderdone*, French *guerdon*, from whence Chaucer took it and made it English. *Vide* Diez, *Romance Dictionary;* Skeat, *Historical Dictionary.*

Line 220.   And all about us pealed the nightingale
        Rapt in *her* song.

It is only the male bird which sings. The functions of the sexes are strictly defined in the land of singing birds. But the poets, all of them, keep the old Greek myth in mind, and while scientifically wrong, are poetically and historically correct, for Philomela was a princess who was turned into a nightingale which sang. Even Isaac Walton uses the pronoun "her." Milton, in *Il Pensersoso*, writes "*Sweet chauntress*," thinking evidently of poor Philomela. Chaucer in the *Cuckow and the Nightingale* uses always the feminine gender—
        I thanked *her*, and was ryght wel apayed;
        Yee, quoth *she*, and be thou not amayed.

Line 229.   Into rooms which *gave*
    Upon a pillared porch.

So also in the *Gardener's Daughter*—
   This, yielding, *gave* into a grassy walk.

And in *Gareth and Lynette*—
   Now two great entries opened from the hall;
   At one end one, that *gave* upon a range
   Of level pavement.

The use of *gave* in this manner is a Gallicism adopted from an idiomatic use of the word *donner*.

Line 243.   The seal was Cupid bent above a scroll,
      And o'er his head *Uranian Venus* hung,
      And raised the blinding bandage from
       his eyes.

The allusion here is to a passage in Plato's *Symposium*:—

"And am I not right in asserting that there are two goddesses? The elder one having no mother, who is called the heavenly Aphrodite—she is the daughter of Uranus; the younger who is the daughter of Zeus and Dione—her we call Common; and the Love, who is her fellow-worker, may and must also have the name of common, as the other love is called heavenly."—*Jowett, Dialogues of Plato*, vol. ii.

CANTO II.

Line 8.   Thro' the porch that *sang*
    All round with laurel.

Laurel—the tree of the god of the lyre. A fragrant tree with abundance of fragrant blossoms, the favourite resort of birds and bees. This porch is suggestive of a passage in Ariosto, vi. 21—

> Small thickets with the scented laurel gay,
>   Cedar and orange, full of fruit and flower.
> Myrtle and palm, with interwoven spray,
>   Pleached in mixed modes, all lovely form a bower.
> And breaking with their shade the scorching ray,
>   Make a cool shelter from the noontide hour,
> And nightingales among those branches wing
> Their flight,—and safely amorous descants sing.

Line 14. *Enringed* a billowing fountain.

The prefix *en* was much used by Shakespeare and the older writers where it is now abandoned. Generally it was employed as here, in its proper sense of surrounding, but sometimes to add force or intensity to a word as the "*enridged sea*," the "*enchafed flood*." In the *Midsummer Night's Dream*, iv. 1, we find—

> The female ivy so
> *Enrings* the barky fingers of the elm.

In *Henry V.*, Prologue to Act iv., a similar word is used—

> How dread an army hath *enrounded* him.

Line 28. Not without *redound*,
Of use and glory to yourselves ye come.

The use of *redound* as a substantive is very rare. It does not occur in Shakespeare, Milton, Chaucer, or elsewhere in Tennyson. It is a sonorous word for the end of a line, and there is no reason why it should not be adopted or retained, as *rebound* and many other similar words.

Line 38. He worships your *ideal*.

A very peculiar sense is given to the word ideal here, and one not found elsewhere. The *ideal* of the Princess, that is her conception of the highest perfection, is not what the

Prince is worshipping. He worships the Princess herself as *his* ideal, and puts one for the other with a confusion of thought pardonable under the circumstances.

Line 65.   She
   That taught the Sabine how to rule.

The second king of Rome, Numa, was a Sabine of the city of Cures. He was believed to have received the laws, both civil and religious, which he instituted at Rome, from the nymph Egeria, whose society he sought in the recesses of the forest of Aricia. After the death of Numa she became inconsolable, and was changed by Diana into a fountain (as related by Ovid, *Meta.* xv.) which may be seen to this day near Lake Nemi.

Line 66.   The foundress of the Babylonian wall.

Semiramis—the queen who is fabled to have founded Babylon. Herodotus says very little about her, but praises Queen Nitocris as having been much wiser, and as having constructed greater works.

Line 67.   The Carian Artemisia, strong in war.

There were two of the name, queens of Caria. This was the first; she joined Xerxes with an admirably equipped squadron, and fought at Salamis so bravely, that Xerxes said his women had become men, and his men women. She escaped, but by the discreditable stratagem of running down a friendly ship. She afterwards fell in love with a young man who did not return her passion, so she put out his eyes and then threw herself into the sea at the Lover's Leap, at the promontory of Leucate. The other Artemisia it was, who, losing her husband Mausolus, built the celebrated tomb, thence called the Mausoleum, and died of grief two years later.

Line 68.   The Rhodope that built the pyramid.

Tennyson has followed a legend common in Greece which has no foundation in fact. Herodotus almost loses his temper at those who believe the story. To begin—the lady's name is given by him as Rhodōpis, not Rhodope, who was a somewhat[1] insignificant water-nymph; but having noted the fact we will follow[2] the pronunciation of the poem. Rhodope, then, was a Thracian slave-girl of great beauty, a fellow-slave with Æsop, and was bought by Xanthus, a Samian. Her master carried her to Egypt in the reign of Amasis and sold her. She was bought by a brother of Sappho the poetess, who became so enamoured of her that he emancipated her to the[3] great indignation of his sister. She settled at Naucratis and became very rich, and the story became current that she built the third pyramid. Ebers, in his beautiful story of "An Egyptian Princess," relates many things of this beautiful and gifted woman. Athenæus also refers to this same person under the name of Doricha.[4] He thinks Herodotus wrong in supposing Doricha and Rhodopis to be the same; but Athenæus was a great gossip, and his authority cannot weigh against that of the careful and accurate "father of history." Pliny[5] believed the story about the pyramid and wonders how she got so much money. Ælian[6] relates it on the authority of the Egyptians, and he accounts for it by a very pretty story. Rhodopis, he says, was bathing, and an eagle snatched up one of her sandals and flying away dropped it in the lap of King Psammeticus as he was sitting in judgment. He wondered at the beauty of the shoe and sent all over Egypt until he found the owner, whom he straightway married. This accounts for the facts, and throws light on the story of Cinderella at the same time.

    [1] Liddell & Scott, ad verbum.
    [2] Bayle—Dict., ad verb.
    [3] Athenæus, vol. iii. p. 951.
    [4] *Ibid.*
    [5] Pliny, Nat. Hist., book 36, cap. 17.
    [6] Ælian, Var. Hist., book 13, cap. 33.

These are pretty stories and are poetically true, but in fact[1] Herodotus must be right. For, as he shows, it was impossible that any private person could have built this pyramid ; and besides, as Rhodopis dedicated the tenth part of her wealth to Apollo at Delphi, any one, he says, can see how inadequate it was. He adds conclusively that the pyramids were built long before the reign of Amasis.

But the glory of the third pyramid still belongs to a woman. This pyramid is the most carefully finished of the three great pyramids, and is sometimes called the Pyramid of Menkeres or Mycerinus. Manĕtho says that it was built by Queen Nitocris, the sister and wife of Menkeres.[2] Menkeres commenced it for his own tomb, and she completed it. This was one or two thousand years before Amasis reigned. The time is a little vague, but Egyptologists, like geologists, are not by any means precise people as to dates. Anyway it was a long time before, and Nitocris reigned twelve years —a queen of great ability and vigour, and a strong conservative, as most clever women are. Her husband was assassinated by the party of progress, and for years she was obliged to temporise with his murderers. But she waited patiently until she got them all quietly as guests at a banquet in the subterranean chambers of some building, when she let the Nile in on them and drowned them. Evidently a dangerously strong-minded lady.[3]

All these stories, diverse in appearance, are easily reconciled, for Rhodōpis is Greek for rosy-cheeked, and Nitocris was a woman of surpassing loveliness.[4] Manetho calls her the "rosy-cheeked beauty." I add the naive conclusion of Herodotus :—" Now I have done speaking of Rhodopis."

Tennyson has followed the example of Shakespeare both in the pronunciation of the word and the main story. See *K. Henry VI.*, 1st Part, Act i. Sc. 6—

[1] Herodotus, ii. 134.
[2] Cory's Ancient Fragments, p. 115.
[3] Herodotus, book ii. cap. 100. Lenormant, Anc. Hist. of East, vol. i. p. 211.
[4] *Ibid.*

A statelier pyramid to her I'll rear,
Than Rhodope's or Memphis' ever was.

Lines 69-71.   Clelia, Cornelia, with the Palmyrene
That fought Aurelian, and the Roman brows
Of Agrippina.

Clœlia, a Roman girl given with others as hostages to Porsenna. She escaped by swimming the Tiber on horseback.
Cornelia, the mother of the Gracchi.
The Palmyrene, Queen Zenobia.
Agrippina, grand-daughter of Augustus. She accompanied her husband Germanicus in his campaigns in Germany. A noble woman in a corrupt age.

Line 73.   Makes noble through the sensuous organism
That which is higher.

The mind, though higher than the body, is ennobled through the senses by the contemplation of noble objects. Shelley has the same thought in *Prince Athanase*—

   The mind becomes that which it contemplates;
   And so Zonoras, by for ever seeing
   Their bright creations, grew like wisest men.

Line 98.   Then Florian, but no livelier than the dame
That whisper'd "Asses' ears" among the sedge.

This is an outright slander. Ovid is the authority for this story about Midas, and he distinctly says it was a barber who was unable to keep the secret. Tennyson follows Chaucer in charging it upon the female sex. Chaucer gives Ovid as his authority, but in all probability he took the story indirectly, as he did many others, from the Italian with which he was very familiar. Tennyson's poetry is pervaded with the influence of Chaucer. The passage alluded to is in the *Wife of Bath's Tale*, line 113—

> And sins sche dorste not tell it unto man,
> Doun to a marreys faste by sche ran,
> Til sche cam ther, hir herte was on fuyre;
> And as a bytoure bumblith in the myre,
> Sche layde hir mouth unto the water doun.
> " Bywrey me not, thou watir, with thi soun,"
> Quod sche, " to the I telle it, and nomo,
> Myn housbond hath long asse eeris tuo.
> Now is myn hert al hool, now is it oute,
> I mighte no lenger kepe it out of doute."

Pope refers probably to Chaucer also, in his *Epistle to Dr. Arbuthnot*, v. 68—

> 'Tis sung, when Midas' ears began to spring
> (Midas, a sacred person and a king),
> His very minister who spied them first
> (*Some say his queen*) was forced to speak or burst.

The fairer sex have too many stories of this sort justly attributed to them to be able to bear this in addition.

Line 114. Appraised the Lycian custom—

Herodotus, i. 173, says—
They have one custom peculiar to themselves, in which they differ from all other nations; for they take their name from their mothers, and not from their fathers, and reckon up ancestry in the female line.

Line 115. Those that lay at wine with Lar and Lucumo.

That is the Etruscan women. Tanaquil, the wife of Tarquinius Priscus was a haughty and high-spirited woman ; a manager of the first order. She in truth made her husband's fortune by removing him to Rome. Her name was a proverb in Rome for a domineering wife. In Etruria women occupied a much superior position than in Greece, and the Romans probably followed the Etrurian custom in this respect. Begoe, an Etruscan woman, wrote a book on divination which became a statute book, and there [1] were women soothsayers and augurs. In the paintings at Volterra the females are represented seated at banquets with their husbands and mixing freely in society. From the same source, we learn that girls were sent to school, and we may argue from the number of rolls in the pupils' hands that the higher education was not neglected. It would be erroneous to suppose that Etruscan society was better than Greek or Roman. It was distinctly worse. The women were extravagantly fond of personal adornment, and Athenæus says they were wonderful women to drink. Their husbands were noted in Italy for being fat and idle.' Altogether the less the ladies say about the Etruscan women the better.[2]

Line 119.　She *fulmined* out her scorn of laws Salique.

A word not much used now, having been superseded by *fulminate*. Milton uses it, *Paradise Regained*, iv. 270—

　　　　　Whose resistless eloquence
Wielded at will that fierce democratie,
Shook the arsenal, and *fulmined* over Greece.

Spenser also uses the word. *Laws Salique* were the laws of the Salian Franks, which still obtain in France and Germany, by which females are excluded from the throne.

[1] Chambers's Papers for People—Art. Sepulchres of Etruria, p. 14.
[2] Athenæus, vol. iii. p. 829—Tyrrhenians he calls them. See also Classical Dict.—Art. Tanaquil, Tarquinius I. ; Virgil, Æneid, book ii. 725 *et seq.* ; Plautus, Cistellaria, Act 3 ; Catullus, xxxix. 11—" Obesus Etruscus."

Line 129.   *Disyoke* their necks from custom.

See note on p. 61. And also *Gareth and Lynette*—
   Until she let me fly *discaged* to sweep
   In ever highering eagle-circles.

And elsewhere in *The Princess*—*disprinced, dishelmed, disrobed.*

Line 137.   Thence the man's ; if more was more.

That is, if a larger brain does really give greater mental power (which she doubts); men have acquired larger brains than women only by constant use, and women's brains would increase in volume under similar conditions.

Line 183.   The softer Adams of your Academe.

The female founders of your university.

Line 206.   Whate'er I was
   Disrooted.

See note on p. 61, on use of *dis* for *un.*

Line 203.   I think no more of deadly lurks therein,
   Than in a *clapper* clapping in a *garth,*
   To scare the fowl from fruit.

A scare-crow in a fruit-garden. *Garth,* an old English word, from which both *garden* and *yard* are derived. The old High German word was *gart,* originally *gard,* hence English *yard,* French *jardin,* English *garden,* Italian *giardino.* Original signification, any enclosed place. The word is uncommon. Tennyson uses it several times, *e.g., Enoch Arden—*
   And fast into the little *garth* beyond.

And in the *Grandmother*—
> I climbed to the top of the *garth*, and stood by the road at the gate.

In Yorkshire the word is in common use to signify any enclosure adjoining a house, as *kirk-garth* for churchyard.

Line 226.　The gaunt old Baron with his *beetle* brow,
　　　　Sun-shaded in the heat of dusty fights.

Shakespeare—*Romeo and Juliet*, i. 4—
> Here are the beetle-brows, shall blush for me.

And *Hamlet*, i. 4—
> The summit of the cliff
> That *beetles* o'er his base into the sea.

Skeat, in his *Etymological Dictionary*, states that Shakespeare coined the verb *to beetle*, *i.e.*, to project, from the word *bitelbrowed*, a Middle English word signifying having projecting or sharp brows. It is from the Anglo-Saxon *bitel*, "the biting insect," and really means with *biting* brows, that is, with brows which project like the upper jaw. The word *beetle*, a heavy mallet, comes from another Anglo-Saxon verb *beatan*, to beat.

Line 270.　The *Lucius Junius Brutus* of my kind.

The Brutus who expelled the Tarquins, and subsequently condemned his sons to death for treason.

Line 312.　And all her thoughts as *fair* within her eyes,
　　　　As bottom agates seen to wave and float
　　　　In crystal currents of clear morning seas.

Fair in the sense of clear, evident, as Shakespeare, *King John*, iv. 1—

>Can you not read it? is it not fair writ?

A parallel passage occurs in Moore—*Loves of the Angels*—

>I soon could track each thought that lay,
>Gleaming within her heart, as clear
>As pebbles within brooks appear.

And also in Beaumont and Fletcher, *The Two Noble Kinsmen*, i. 1—

>You cannot read it there; there through my tears,
>Like wrinkled pebbles in a glassy stream,
>You may behold them.

Line 326.   For fear
>This whole foundation *ruin*.

A very unusual use of *ruin* as an intransitive verb.

CANTO III.

Line 35. You need not set your thoughts in rubric thus

>For *wholesale* comment.

A very odd use of a modern mercantile word.

Line 69. And *still* she railed against the state of things.

Still in the sense of continually, habitually. As Canto i. 57—

>For *still* we moved
>Together, twinned as horses' ear and eye.

A use common in the poets and early writers.

Line 75. Consonant chords that shiver to one
                    note ;
            One mind in all things.

A similar thought is found in Shelley—*Epipsychidion*—
   Are we not formed, as notes of music are,
   For one another, though dissimilar?

But Tennyson's simile is more full of meaning. The notes are not only made for one another, but, being chords, blend into one musical note, and the ear cannot separate the two sets of vibrations.

Line 91.   But I
        An eagle *clang* an eagle to the sphere.
And again, Canto iv., line 416—
        The leader wild-swan in among the stars
        Would *clang* it.

This use of *clang* as a transitive verb is peculiar to Tennyson. It is the far-sounding scream of the eagle soaring sunwards which is contrasted with the chatter of the crane in the preceding lines. It is a very expressive word, and its present use is an adaptation of the Greek and Latin use of the same root-verb.

Line 105. And leaning there on those *balusters* high.

Baluster, accented on the penult: from French *balustre*, now corrupted into *bannister*.

Line 106.   Drank the gale
        That, blown about the foliage underneath,
        And sated with the innumerable rose,
        Beat balm upon our eyelids.

A parallel passage occurs in Shelley—*Epipsychidion*—
>The light clear element, which the isle wears,
>Is heavy with the scent of lemon flowers,
>Which floats like mist laden with unseen showers,
>And falls upon the eyelids like faint sleep.

Line 113. Better to clear *prime* forests.

For primeval, as Shakespeare, *Rich. III.*, iv. 3—
>That from the *prime* creation.

Or in the original sense of *primus*, first.

Line 122. I fabled nothing *fair*
But your example pilot, told her all.

That is, I did not invent a plausible story; *fair* for *fair-seeming*, plausible. Used in that sense in the proverb "*fair* and false."

Line 161. Beyond the thick-leaved *platans* of the vale.

Plátanus, the plane-tree.

Line 181. Went forth in long *retinue*, following up
The river as it narrowed to the hills.

Retínue—accented on the penult—also in Aylmer's *Field*—
>The dark *retínue* reverencing death.

So Milton, *Par. Lost*, v. 355—
>On princes, when their rich *retínue* long.

And Shakespeare, *Lear*, i. 4—
>But other of your insolent *retínue*.

But Chaucer follows the French *retenue*, accenting on the last syllable, *Frere's Tale*, 57—

  And he had wenches at his retenue.

This is an instance of the constant tendency in English to throw back the accent.

Line 217. "Alas! your Highness breathes full East," I said.

Referring to the dry unpleasant east-winds prevalent in England, supposed by the hypochondriac islanders to parch up everything.

Line 249. Who learns the one Pou Sto whence after-hands
  May move the world.

The Princess is quoting the celebrated saying of Archimedes to King Hiero. That philosopher was a master of all the arts of applied mechanics, and dwelling on the enormous mechanical powers of the lever he exclaimed, "Give me *where I may stand* (pou sto), and I will move the world."

Line 264. Cramped under worse than South-sea isle *taboo*.

This word was brought home by Captain Cook's expedition. The South Sea islands were under the domination of a priesthood, which reserved to its own use anything which any of the members of its class might fancy, by marking it and calling it *taboo*, or devoted to religious uses.

Line 283.   "Dare we dream of that," I asked,
  "Which wrought us, as the workman and his work,
  "That practice betters."

Dare we suppose that the Being who created us is like a human workman who improves by practice?

Line 288.   Diotima teaching him that died Of hemlock.

Diotima was a wise woman of Mantinea who instructed Socrates in many things. Lucian[1] twice mentions her name in company with that of Aspasia, but we should have known nothing about her had it not been that Plato in the *Symposium* makes Socrates call her his instructress. She was evidently in Athens when Socrates learned of her, for he calls her, "O thou stranger woman." He describes her as wise in many branches of knowledge, and says that the plague at Athens was deferred ten years by a sacrifice she made. She was his teacher in the art of love, and that of the loftiest kind, for he makes her define love as the "love of the everlasting possession of the good."

Line 296.   These monstrous males that carve the living hound,
              And cram him with the fragments of the grave.

Referring to the practice of vivisection and the brutal irreverence which is charged against those who practise it, as shown by the custom sometimes asserted to exist of feeding dogs with the fragments of the dissecting room. The poet still retains his horror of vivisection. *Vide* "In the Children's Hospital" in his last volume—

I could think he was one of those who would break their jests on the dead,
And mangle the living dog that had loved him and fawned at his knee—
Drenched with the 'hellish oorali—that ever such things should be !

[1] Lucian—The Eunuch ; The Portrait.

In one of Hogarth's series of *The Four Stages of Cruelty* is a print which may have suggested this passage. It represents a dissecting-table at Surgeons' Hall, upon which a subject is stretched out, and dogs are eating the intestines, which are falling upon the floor.

Line 328.
"For indeed these fields
Are lovely, lovelier not the Elysian lawns,
Where paced the demigods of old, and saw
The soft white vapour streak the crowned towers
Built to the sun."

The reference here is evidently to the city and plains of Troy, as will appear on reading the first fourteen lines of *Œnone*. In the same poem the walls of Ilion are pictured as rising and taking shape to the sound of music.

As yonder walls
Rose slowly to a music slowly breathed,
A cloud that gathered shape.

The poet has followed Ovid (*Heroides*, xv. 179), who makes the walls and lofty towers of Ilion rise to the potent melody of Apollo's lyre. Virgil ascribes the building of Ilion to Neptune, but the complete story relates that both these deities assisted. Troy was afterwards taken by Hercules, and the hero demigods his companions. Virgil, x. 469, is suggested by this passage. Jupiter, implored by Hercules to rescue Pallas from the spear of Turnus, replies—"Beneath the tall towers of Troy how many of the sons of the gods fell? Yea, there fell too Sarpedon, my own son."

NOTES. 85

This myth would seem to be a favourite one with Tennyson. In *Tithonus* is another reference to it—

> Like that strange song I heard Apollo sing
> While Ilion like a mist rose into towers.

In like manner rose the city of Camelot. See *Gareth and Lynette*, where it is said of the Fairy Queens, that

> They came from out a sacred mountain-cleft
> Toward the sunrise, each with harp in hand,
> And built it to the music of their harps.

Line 335. A tent of satin elaborately wrought
With fair Corinna's triumph.

Corinna was a Theban poetess, who took the palm five times from Pindar, who is

> The bearded victor of ten thousand hymns

in the following lines. She was very beautiful, and some say, so beautiful that Pindar had no chance of success with the too susceptible judges. Ælian (xiii. 45) says she succeeded because the auditors were ignorant. Pausanias saw a picture of her binding her head with laurel.

CANTO IV.

Line 21   Tears, idle tears, I know not what they mean.

It is difficult to write without enthusiasm of this exquisitely perfect lyric. The rhythm and cadence are so absolutely faultless that the absence of rhyme is not noticed in reading. The thoughts of women naturally dwell much more on the past than in the future; and Violet the singer has not much sympathy with the radical reforms dreamed of by the Princess. Her song is a sweet utterance of unconscious feminine protest against the new revolutionary doctrines, and jars on the Princess, who resents it at once.

The idea of this lyric had been resting in the poet's mind since 1831. Then at the age of twenty-two he published in *The Gem*, one of the annuals at that time in fashion, the following poem omitted from all the recent editions of his works—

> O sad *No more!* O sweet *No more!*
>   O strange *No more!*
> By a mossed brookbank on a stone
> I smelt a wildwood flower alone;
> There was a ringing in my ears,
> And both my eyes gushed out with tears,
> Surely all pleasant things had gone before,
> Low-buried fathom deep beneath with thee,
>   *No more!*

The melancholy melody of the refrain "No more" has evidently haunted the poet's mind, and he has taken the poem which he justly suppressed as unworthy of him, and after long years reproduced it in this glorified form. There is nothing like it in English save Keats's *Ode to a Nightingale*. In that poem the word "forlorn" has evidently charmed the ear of the poet in the same manner.

Edgar Allan Poe, in his *Philosophy of Composition*, has explained how a poem may grow up round a musical refrain, and would have us to believe that his poem *The Raven* grew up around the word "Nevermore." *The Raven* is not a poem to be compared with either of the two above mentioned, nor is Poe a writer to be trusted when a theory has once possessed him, but the passage we quote is curious as throwing some light on the possible growth of "Tears, idle tears." Poe says—" Having made up my mind to a refrain, the division of the poem into stanzas was, of course, a corollary, the refrain forming the close to each stanza. That such a close, to have force, must be sonorous and susceptible of protracted emphasis, admitted no doubt; and these considerations inevitably led me to the long *o* as the most sonorous vowel, in connection with *r* as the most producible consonant.

"The sound of the refrain being thus determined, it became necessary to select a word embodying the sound, and at the same time in the fullest possible keeping with that melancholy which it had predetermined as the tone of the poem. In such a search it would have been absolutely impossible to overlook the word 'Nevermore.' In fact it was the very first which presented itself."

It is not credible that poets work consciously in so mechanical a way; or that *o* and *r* should have been the nucleus of a poem; but it is credible, that the associations clustering round an organised and musical word such as *no more* or *nevermore* should suggest the idea of a poem.

Line 59. Let be
Their cancelled Babels; tho' the rough *kex* break
The starred mosaic, and the *beard-blown* goat
Hang on the shaft, and the wild fig-tree split
Their monstrous idols.

Kex—the rough dry husk or stalk of rampant growing weeds. *Beard-blown*—blown by the wind, as the goat stands on some ruined column. *See* Preface, xiv.

The Princess is combating the vague regretful sentiment which Violet's song, "Tears, idle tears," has stirred in the susceptible minds of her students. She is saying in effect, let the dead past bury its dead—let throne after throne, system after system, melt away in the ocean like icebergs from the North. All things have their day, and it is foolish to moan for them. Act! act! in the living present—let the past be past. Let the old unjust world crumble like the buildings of Babel once so lofty. Let the rank weeds break the gay mosaics of the floors—let the goats clamber over the ruined arches—let the fig-tree split the marbles with its vigorous roots—unmourned by me; for they tell of a monstrous system of injustice. We will look forward towards that great year of equal mights and rights when woman will be the equal of man.

The rending power of the wild fig-tree—*Caprificus*—was a trite theme of Roman poets. Martial (x. 2.) thinks his fame will last through his writings while the wild fig splits the monument of Messalæ—

> Marmora Messalæ findit caprificus.

In Horace (*Ep.* v. 17) Canidia makes use of fig-trees plucked from tombs—"Jubet sepulcris caprificos erutas." Juvenal (x. 147), speaking of the vanity of ambition, says—

> Vain rage—the roots of the wild fig-tree rise,
> Strike through the marble, and their memory dies.

Ramage in his *Nooks and By-ways of Italy* (p. 69) is reminded of this passage by noticing a wild fig springing out of, and splitting a rock in the Apennines.

The goat hanging on the shaft suggests, or has been suggested by, Shelley's Preface to *Prometheus Unbound*. He says, "This poem was chiefly written upon the mountainous ruins of the baths of Caracalla among the flowery glades and thickets of odoriferous blossoming trees which are extended in ever-winding labyrinths upon its immense platforms and dizzy arches suspended in the air." The passage is very suggestive of these ruins, the mosaic floors are riven by rank weeds, and the lofty arches break the blue sky with fragile and giddy bridges which only a goat dare tread upon.

Wace[1] says "Kex" is the provincial word for hemlock. Skeat (*Etymological Dictionary*) gives—Kex, hemlock; a hollow stem (Celtic); Provincial English, kecksies. Kex is itself plural=kecks; and kecksies is a double plural. The precise meaning of the word in this passage is given in Shakespeare, *Henry V.* v. 2—

> Such savagery;
> The even mead, that erst brought sweetly forth
> The freckled cowslip, burnet, and green clover,
> Wanting the scythe, all uncorrected rank,
> Conceives by idleness; and nothing teems,
> But hateful docks, rough thistles, kecksies, burs,
> Losing both beauty and utility.

A picture of the wasted land of France after the long war. Kex—pl. kecksies—does not mean hemlock here, for the third line previous reads—

> The darnel, hemlock, and rank fumitory.

In the country parts of England the word *kecks* is still in use. In Leicestershire it means the dry stalks of almost any worthless weed. "As dry as kecks" is a common phrase in Wiltshire.

Line 69.   Not a Death's head at the wine.

Allusion is here made to a custom of the ancient Egyptians recorded by Herodotus (i. 78): "At their convivial banquets, among the wealthy classes, when they have finished supper, a man carries round in a coffin the image of a dead body carved in wood, made as like as possible in colour and workmanship, and in size generally about one or two cubits in length; and showing this to each of the company, he says, 'Look upon this, then drink and enjoy yourself; for when dead you will be like this.' This practice they have at their drinking parties."

---

[1] Alfred Tennyson; his Life and Works, p. 120.

Line 84. Oh were I thou, that she might take me in,
  And lay me on her bosom, and her heart
  Would rock the snowy cradle till I died.

This is evidently a reminiscence of Shakespeare—*Venus and Adonis*, last stanza but one—

  Lo, in this hollow cradle take thy rest,
  My throbbing heart shall rock thee day and night.

Line 100. Like the Ithacensian suitors in old time,
  Stared with great eyes *and laughed with alien lips.*

The reference is to the *Odyssey*, xx. 347. The suitors at the court of Penelope feel the occult influence of the unseen goddess Pallas causing their thoughts to wander. They fail to recognise Ulysses in his disguise, and their laughter is constrained and unnatural, they know not why. They *laugh with alien lips,* which is the nearest possible poetical translation of the Greek idiomatic expression, "They laughed with other men's *jaws.*"

Line 103. "Not for thee," she said,
  "O *Bulbul,* any rose of *Gulistan*
  Shall burst her veil; *marsh-divers,* rather, maid,
  Shall croak thee sister, or the *meadow-crake*
  Grate her harsh kindred in the grass."

The nightingale is the *Bulbul* in Persia, and Persian poets feign that he is the constant lover of the rose, to whom he pours out his passionate melodies. *Gulistan* is Persian for rose-garden. Saadi calls his book of poems—Gulistan. The Princess does not think that any rose-bud would open at the singing of such a nightingale as the Prince. Marsh-divers—probably the water-rail, is meant. Meadow-crake—the corn-crake or land-rail. Says Wood, "The cry of the corn-crake may be exactly imitated by drawing a quill or a piece of stick smartly over the large teeth of a comb, or by rubbing together two jagged strips of bone." The Princess is severe on the singers. Neither the matter of the one, or the manner of the other, pleases her.

Line 130.   Whole in ourselves, and *owed* to none.

As an intransitive verb in the sense of, to be bound; a rare use, but found in Chaucer.

Line 185.   Of open-work in which the hunter rued
His rash intrusion, manlike, but his brows
Had sprouted.

The allusion is to the hunter Actæon, who, having come upon Diana and her nymphs when bathing, was turned into a stag.

Line 236.   He has a solid base of temperament;
But as the water-lily starts and slides
Upon the level in little puffs of wind
Tho' anchor'd to the bottom, such is he.

A very similar passage occurs in Wordsworth—*Excursion*, book v., where it is said of Moral Truth that it is—

>   A thing
> Subject, you deem, to vital accidents,
> And, like the water-lily, lives and thrives,
> Whose root is fix'd in stable earth, whose head
> Floats on the tossing waves.

Wordsworth's is the more familiar picture. This parallel passage has been noticed by Mr. Wace.

Line 243.
> But I began
> To thrid the *musky-circled* mazes, wind
> And double in and out the *boles.*

Musky-circled mazes, garden walks with fragrant borders. Musky is used by Milton in the sense of fragrant in Comus—

> And west winds with musky wing,
> About the cedarn alleys fling
> Nard and Cassia's balmy smells.

Bole, the stem of a tree; a word much used by Tennyson, but not found in Shakespeare, Milton, or Chaucer. It is frequently heard in the northern and central districts of England, sometimes spelt *boll,* as *thorn-boll,* but usually pronounced *bool.*

Line 255.
> Above her drooped a lamp,
> And made the single jewel on her brow
> Burn like the *mystic fire* on a masthead,
> Prophet of storm.

When the atmosphere is in a state of electrical tension, brush-shaped or star-like flames are seen on the masts of ships, or on pointed objects on land. Mariners call them St. Elmo's fires. The real name of the saint was Erasmus of Formia. He is venerated in Southern Italy under the corrupted name of St. Elmo. Sailors invoke his aid in time of storm, and the appearance of St. Elmo's fires is thought to be of good omen. The Greeks and Romans ascribed these appearances to Castor and Pollox. So Macaulay, *Battle of Lake Regillus*—

> Safe comes the ship to haven,
> Through billows and through gales,
> If once the Great Twin Brethren
> Sit shining on the sails.

Line 260.   Huge women *blowzed* with health, and wind, and rain.

Blowsed, swarthy. Shakespeare, *Titus Andronicus*, iv. 2—

Sweet *blowse*, you are a beauteous blossom sure.

Said of a swarthy child—the son of the Moor Aaron and the Queen of the Goths. In the Kentish dialect a great *blowze* means a red-faced wench.

Line 420.   Sphered up with Cassiopeia, or the enthroned Persephone in Hades.

Cassiopeia, queen of Ethiopia, now one of the chief constellations in the northern sky. Persephone or Proserpine, the daughter of Ceres, and queen of Hades.

Line 424.   Not in this *frequence* can I lend full tongue.

Frequence is the older and original meaning of throng, as in Milton, *Par. Reg.* i. 128—

> Who in full *frequence* bright,
> Of angels, thus to Gabriel smiling spake.

Line 427.   That many a famous man and woman, town,
    And *landskip,* have I heard of.

This is the old and correct spelling. The word, says Skeat, is undoubtedly derived from the Dutch painters, and answers nearly to the word background. It is a Dutch word, *land-schap,* and means a province or extent of land. *Schap* answers to the Anglo-Saxon *ship* in friendship, lordship. *Sch* is harder in Dutch than in English, hence the *sk* in *landskip.* Milton usually spells the word thus, as in *Par. Lost,* v. 142—

    Discovering in wild landskip all the East.

Line 475.   Fixt like a beacon tower above the waves
    Of tempest, when the crimson rolling eye
    Glares ruin, and the wild birds on the light
    Dash themselves dead.

The same simile occurs in *Enoch Arden*—
    Allured him as the beacon-blaze allures
    The bird of passage, till he madly strikes
    Against it, and beats out his weary life.

The description in the first passage is far more vivid. The lofty tower, the tempest, and the red revolving light intensify the picture. A parallel passage occurs in Longfellow—*The Lighthouse*—

    The sea-bird wheeling round it, with the din
        Of wings and winds and solitary cries,

> Blinded and maddened by the light within,
> Dashes himself against the glare and dies.

But Longfellow's poem was published in 1849, two years after *The Princess*.

INTERLUDE BETWEEN CANTOS IV. AND V.

Thy voice is heard thro' rolling drums.

Another version of this song is given in a volume of selections made by Tennyson, although not published in his collected works.

> Lady, let the rolling drums
> Beat to battle where thy warrior stands :
> Now thy face across his fancy comes,
> And gives the battle to his hands.
>
> Lady, let the trumpets blow,
> Clasp thy little babes about thy knee :
> Now their warrior father meets the foe,
> And strikes him dead for thine and thee.

The version finally adopted is by far the better of the two.

CANTO V.

Line 2.   We stumbled on a *stationary* voice.

The voice of one *stationed* at a post—a sentinel. In French, *soldats stationnaires* are guards detached singly; from the post-classical *stationarii milites*. This use of the word is a Latinism.

96   NOTES.

Line 26.　　　　　　　Or a draggled *mawkin* thou
　　　　　That tends her bristled grunters in the
　　　　　　sludge.

Mawkin. Used in the country parts of England to mean a cloth tied to the end of a pole for sweeping out the bottom of an oven, and thence applied to any slovenly woman. Used also in this sense in *The Last Tournament*—

　　　For when had Lancelot uttered aught so gross
　　　Ev'n to the swineherd's *malkin* in the mast?

Mawkin and *malkin* would appear to be different forms of the same word, as Shakespeare—*Coriolanus*, ii. 1—

　　　　　　　　The kitchen *malkin* pins
　　　Her richest lockram 'bout her reechy neck.

It is, however, asserted by some that *malkin* is a diminutive of Mary, like Molly, and means a wench—a servant-girl.

Line 39.　Away we stole, and *transient* in a trice.

A Latinism, *transient* is used as a present participle, signifying passing from one condition to another.

Line 93.　*Ill* mother that I was to leave her there.

Ill in the sense of bad, as used by Shakespeare and retained in a few common expressions, as *ill* luck, *ill* health.

Line 193.　My mother looks as *whole* as some
　　　　　　serene
　　　　　Creation.

The word *whole* is used throughout the poem, and generally by Tennyson in the sense of complete and entire.

Line 260.   Like those three stars of the *airy Giant's zone*,
That glitter burnished by the *frosty dark*.

The three stars in the Belt of Orion. In the winter months this constellation with its many brilliant stars, and Sirius, the brightest of the fixed stars, are the chief ornaments of the southern heavens at night.

Line 263.   And as the *fiery* Sirius *alters hue*,
And *bickers* into red and emerald, shone
Their morions, washed with morning, as they came.

Fiery Sirius—the dog-star.   Sirius ardor ille.—Virgil, *Æneid*, x. 273. Fervidus ille Canis.—Aratus in Cicero, *Nat. Deorum*, 11-44. It is described as a *red* star by Ptolemy and Seneca. Aratus calls it many-coloured. Lockyer, *Elem. Lessons*, p. 24, says it is *green*, but in his work entitled *Stargazing*, p. 351, he says it is *white*. When highest in the heavens it unquestionably appears white, but its altitude is never very great, and when low down on the horizon sailors notice the change of colour referred to by the poet, and ascribe it correctly to atmospheric influences. Sirius has always been remarkable for scintillation, due probably to its great brightness. Sailors in ancient times observed all such things very closely, and Tennyson is following Homer, as will appear by some remarks on this passage in Proctor's *Myths and Marvels of Astronomy*, p. 166 :—

" Every bright star when close to the horizon shows these colours, and so much the more distinctly as the star is the brighter. Sirius, which surpasses the brightest stars of the northern hemisphere full four times in lustre, shows these changes of colour so conspicuously that they were regarded as specially characteristic of this star, insomuch that Homer speaks of Sirius (not by name, but as the 'Star of Autumn') shining most beautifully 'when laved of ocean's wave'—that is, when close to the horizon."

The expression "laved of ocean's wave" explains the "washed with morning" of our poet. The glitter of the early morning sun on the bright helmets of the brothers, and the glance of light upon their armour as they rode, are vividly realised in this beautiful simile.

The passage of Homer referred to is *Iliad*, v. 5, and is thus rendered by Merivale—

> Flashed from his helm and buckler a bright incessant gleam,
> Like summer's star, that burns afar, new bathed in ocean's stream.

And by Lord Derby—

> Forth from his helm and shield a fiery light
> There flashed, like autumn's star, that brightest shines
> When newly risen from his ocean bath.

The rendering *summer* star is beyond question the more correct. It is the star which is in the ascendant at the *time of ripening*, that is, during the *dog-days*. The autumn is the time of harvesting the corn which has been ripened.

Line 294.   Her that talked down the fifty wisest
    men ;
    She was a princess too.

St. Catherine of Alexandria, the Catherine usually painted with a wheel, or with a book, or disputing with philosophers. The patron saint of philosophy, a legendary saint, the daughter of King Costis, who was the son of Constantius Chlorus, the father of Constantine by a first marriage.

Costis married Sabinella, Queen of Egypt, and on his death Catherine became Queen. She devoted herself to learning, and would not marry, but was espoused in a vision to Jesus Christ. Maxentius during his persecution sent fifty of the wisest philosophers to convert her, but she converted them out of the Law and Prophets, Plato, Aristotle, and the Sibylline books. Unable to kill her with the wheel, Maxentius cut off her head, and the angels carried her body to heaven. The French say she is the patron saint of old maids, because it requires so much philosophy to remain an old maid.

Line 377. Of lands in which at the altar the poor bride
Gives her harsh groom for bridal-gift a scourge;
Of living hearts that crack within the fire
Where smoulder their dead despots.

Allusion is made in the first two lines to Russian customs in the seventeenth century. One was that the bride, on her wedding day, should present her husband, in token of submission, with a whip made by her own hands. Another was, that on arriving at the nuptial chamber the bridegroom ordered the bride to pull off his boots. In one was a whip, in the other a trinket. If she pulled off the one with the whip first the groom gave her a slight blow. It is worthy of note, that according to Bracton a wife is *sub virga*, under the rod, and Blackstone says that moderate correction with a stick is lawful.

The last two lines refer to the Hindoo *Suttee*, now abolished, in conformity with which widows were burned upon the funeral pyres of their husbands.

Line 445. When the man wants weight, the woman takes it up,
And topples down the scales.

The hard old king has stated a fact known to all observers of the genus *homo;* but he has also uttered a scientific truth, which, according to an eminent scientific lady, Dr. Antoinette Brown Blackwell, is applicable to all the animal kingdom. She says (*Sexes throughout Nature*, p. 85):—

"Conversely, among a few species of birds in several orders, the males take upon themselves the duties of incubation and the feeding of the young, and, as it should be upon our hypothesis, the sexes in these cases effect a complete exchange of many characters. In an Australian species of the Turnix, the females are nearly twice as large as the males. In an Indian species the male wants the black on the throat and neck, and the whole tone of the plumage is lighter and less pronounced than that of the female. The females are more vociferous, more pugnacious, and it is they, and not the males, who are kept like game-cocks for fighting. After laying their eggs, the females associate in flocks and leave the males to sit on them." In the case of these birds it is the females who go to the club.

The learned lady goes on translating the old king's sentiments into evolutionary language thus (p. 96) :—

"Whenever brilliantly-coloured male birds have acquired something of maternal habits, tastes and impulses, conversely, the females seem always to have acquired some counterbalancing weight of male character." (How precise our poet was—his very words !) "They are large in relative size, are brilliantly coloured, are active and quarrelsome, or are a little of all these together. The large majority of birds illustrate this law."

Decidedly an unpleasant prospect this, seeing that in a ball-room the fact is evident that already the male portion of our species have lost the gay attire they used to wear in former centuries. The soberly-dressed hum-drum business man, furrowed with care of shop and stocks, is outshone everywhere by his partner of the other sex. In truth males of the human species are tending to follow the sad-coloured males of the cassowaries who hatch the eggs their gadding spouses lay. Mrs. Blackwell seems to be right, but then the dreadful result of the law! "The females are active, quarrelsome, and pugnacious." This reconciles one to the "approaching end of the age."

Line 503.   He rode the *mellay*, lord of the ringing lists.

Mellay for the more usual *melée*, from the verb to mell, *i.e.*, to meddle, to mix, used by Spenser. The confused crowd of combatants after the first charge at a tournament.

CANTO VI.

The opening song,
　　　　Home they brought her warrior dead,

is probably a later version or adaptation of a song first published in a volume of selections issued in 1865, and which is not found in most of the editions of Tennyson's collected works.

　　　Home they brought him slain with spears.
　　　　They brought him home at even-fall;
　　　All alone she sits and hears
　　　　Echoes in his empty hall,
　　　　　　　Sounding on the morrow.

　　　The sun peeped in from open field,
　　　　The boy began to leap and prance,
　　　Rode upon his father's lance,
　　　　Beat upon his father's shield,
　　　　　　　"Oh hush, my joy, my sorrow."

This song may have been suggested by a passage in Scott —*Lay of the Last Minstrel*, canto i.—

> But o'er her warrior's bloody bier
>   The Ladye dropped nor flower nor tear !
> Vengeance deep-brooding o'er the slain
>   Had locked the source of softer woe,
> And burning pride and high disdain
>   Forbade the rising tear to flow;
> Until, amid his sorrowing clan,
>   Her son lisped from the nurse's knee—
> " And if I live to be a man,
>   My father's death revenged shall be."
> Then fast the mother's tears did seek
> To dew the infant's kindling cheek.

The result is the same, but the motive ascribed by Tennyson is more natural and womanly. This passage is an instance of unconscious imitation.

Line 15.   But high upon the palace Ida stood
              With Psyche's *babe in arm.*

The same expression is used in *The Palace of Art*—

> Or the maid-mother by a crucifix,
>   In tracts of pasture sunny warm,
> Beneath branch-work of costly sardonyx
>   Sat smiling *babe in arm.*

The reviewers of Tennyson's earlier poems ridiculed this expression unmercifully, comparing it with the "lance in rest" of the romances of chivalry. Some of their criticisms the poet seems to have accepted as just, for he modified the passages complained of, but this phrase he not only retained but has repeated.

Line 16.   Like that great dame of Lapidoth she
              sang.

Judges iv. 4 : Deborah the prophetess who judged Israel, and who delivered the chosen people from the army of Sisera.

Line 65.   And over them *the tremulous isles of light* slided.

Spots of sunlight through overarching trees—tremulous by the movement of the leaves. *See* Preface, xiv.

Line 122.   And reach its *fatling* innocent arms
And lazy lingering fingers.

Fatling, a diminutive of *fat*, as *suckling* of *suck*. The word is rare as an adjective. Shakespeare uses the older form of the verb *to fat*. It is also met with in Luke xv. 23, the *fatted* calf. *To fatten* is a later form.

Line 126.   Ceased all *on tremble ;* piteous was the cry.

An early English form. The *a* in the words *alive, afoot, asleep,* is a contraction of the Anglo-Saxon *on,* as *on line, on foot.* In Chaucer's *Dream* we find *on sleep*—

Not all wakyng, we fall *on sleepe ;*

and in *Acts* xiii. 36 is another instance—"For David, after he had served his own generation by the will of God, fell *on sleep.*"

Line 185.   When I felt
Thy helpless warmth about my barren breast
In the dead *prime.*

The hour of *prime* is at sunrise. If infants have any regular hour of waking it is with the first dawn; but probably the word here means any hour after midnight.

Line 194.   With an eye that *swum* in thanks.

Shakespeare writes *swam* and even *has swam*, but Milton always *swum*.   *Par. Lost*, ii. 753—

        Dim thine eyes and dizzy *swum*
In darkness.

And *Par. Lost*, xi. 743—

        The floating vessel *swum*
Uplifted, and secure with beaked prow
Rode tilting o'er the waves.

Line 206.   The woman is so hard
    Upon the woman.

This unamiable trait results from woman's mission as the conservator of society. In this respect, woman's character is very narrow, but she feels instinctively that she cannot afford to be lax in offences against social laws. Psyche's weakness had in fact broken up Ida's university, and sins against the family tend to break up society.

Line 286.   Yourself and yours shall have
    Free *adit*.

Access. A rare use of the word. As a mining term it is common.

CANTO VII.

Opening Song.   I strove against the stream, and all in vain.

See Shakespeare, *Venus and Adonis*, for a similar line—
And all in vain you strive against the stream.

There is a song by Thomas Carew, consisting of four stanzas, and commencing with "Ask me no more." That is, however, the only point in common with this poem, as may be seen from the first stanza—

> Ask me no more where June bestows,
> When June is past, the fading rose;
> Nor in your beauties, orient deep,
> These flowers, as in their causes, sleep.

Line 16.   **But oft**
    Clomb to the roofs, and gazed alone for hours.

The old form of the past of *climb:* Chaucer, *House of Fame*—

> But up I *clomb* with all payne.

Line 19.   *Void* was her *use.*

Deprived of her customary occupation. A similar expression occurs in Aylmer's *Field* :—

> So that the gentle creature, *shut from all*
> *Her charitable use*, and face to face
> With twenty months of silence, slowly lost,
> Nor greatly cared to lose her hold on life.

Line 108.   The women up in wild revolt, and stormed
    At the O.ppian law.

This was a sumptuary law passed during the time of the direst distress of Rome, when Hannibal was almost at the gates. It enacted that no woman should wear a gay-coloured dress, or have more than a half an ounce of gold ornaments, and that none should approach within a mile of any city or town in a car drawn by horses. The war being concluded, and the emergency over, the women demanded the repeal of the law. They gained one consul, but Cato, the other one, resisted. The women rose, thronged the streets and forum, and harassed the magistrates until the law was repealed.

Line 112.   Hortensia spoke against the tax.

A heavy tax imposed on Roman matrons by the second triumvirate. No man was found bold enough to oppose it; but Hortensia, daughter of Hortensius, the celebrated orator, spoke so eloquently against it, that her oration was preserved to receive the praise of Quintilian. She was successful.

Line 147.   And left her woman, lovelier in her *mood*,
   Than in her *mould* that other, when she came
   From barren deeps to conquer all with love.

Left her more attractive in the restored sweetness of her womanly moral nature than was Aphrodite rising from the sea in all the splendour of her merely physical perfection.

Line 165.   Now droops the milk-white peacock like a ghost.

Darwin, in his *Animals and Plants under Domestication*, vol. i. p. 305, speaks of a white variety of peacock. This is not a sport, but a permanent variety white from the shell. The peacock always roosts high at night, and preferably in covert places. The drooping tail of a white peacock would look very uncanny on a dark night. The simile is not a happy one, however.

Line 188.   Or fox-like in the vine.

A reminiscence of the Song of Solomon. "Take me the foxes, the little foxes, that spoil the vines." Or of Theocritus more probably, Idyll I., "Two foxes, one is roaming up and down the rows spoiling the ripe grapes."

Line 189.   Walk
    With death and morning on the silver
            horns.

This small sweet Idyll commencing—"Come down, O maid," is one of the most finished passages of the poem. "It transfers," says Symonds (*Greek Poets*, vol. ii.), "with perfect taste, the Greek Idyllic feeling to Swiss scenery; it is a fine instance of new wine being successfully poured into old bottles, for nothing could be fresher, and not even the Thalysia is sweeter." The shepherd is calling his love from the chill and barren, though lofty and beautiful heights, down into the fruitful and smiling valleys of practical life, where she may find happiness by imparting it, and by sharing its duties. The meaning of this line is not clear; but it seems to be a description of the appearance of those lofty Alpine peaks (Matter-horn—Aar-horn—Forister-horn—Alatsch-horn), called in Switzerland "horns" in the early morning before the sun lights them with a ruddy glow. In the early light they have a chill ashen hue as of deathly pallor. The line may be paraphrased into "On the high Alpine summits when they look chill in the early morning." Morning, as portrayed by the poets, is usually rosy or ruddy, but the very earliest dawns of fine mornings are of cool grey tints. Shakespeare and Milton so describe them. As in *Il Penseroso*—
        Civil suited morn.
Or in *Hamlet*, i. 1—
        Morn in russet mantle clad.

And in *Romeo and Juliet*, iii. 5—

> I'll say—yon grey is not the morning's eye.

And in *Julius Cæsar*, ii. 1—

> Yon grey lines
> That fret the clouds are messengers of day.

These cold tints on the snowy Alpine peaks when, as in *Œnone*—

> Far up, the solitary morning smote
> The streaks of virgin snow;

have suggested the words *silver horns* and *death* in an early morning landscape.

Line 249. Stays all the fair young planet in her hands.

It is difficult to discover the astronomical allusion here, or what the precise appropriateness of the word *planet* may be when used to signify the young generation of mankind. Evidently the poet means to say that the influence of the mothers of any given generation of men shape the course of the world during that generation.

Line 256. Will leave her space to *burgeon* out of all Within her.

From the French *bourgeonner*, to put forth buds or young shoots. Found in Middle English, as *borjoune*, a bud.

THE EPILOGUE.

Line 76. Fill me with a faith;
This fine old world of ours is but a child
Yet in the go-cart.

This strong faith runs through all of Tennyson's poems, causing them to be true "medicines for the mind." It is met in the earlier poems, especially in the *Golden Year*, and in the conclusion of *Locksley Hall*, in the poems of middle age as here, and in No. 125 of *In Memoriam*, and in the very last published volume—as Stanza iii. of the *Children's Hospital*, and the Sonnet to *Victor Hugo*. This healthful hope pervading all his writings is one of the secrets of the poet's popularity and influence.

CHANGES AND OMISSIONS.

It has been stated in the preliminary essay that great changes were made in the poem of *The Princess* in the way of additions; and, of these, the most important were noticed. There are, however, some omissions which are worthy of note. In the following passages the lines in italics have been entirely omitted from the final edition.

Canto V., *Line* 116.

You have spoilt the child; she laughs at you and man:
She shall not legislate for Nature, king.

Line 135.

More soluble is the knot,
Like almost all the rest if men were wise.

NOTES.

Line 138.

Your cities into shards with catapults
And dusted down your domes with mangonels.

Line 151.

Tut, you know them not, the girls,
They prize hard knocks and to be won by force.

Line 418.

With claim on claim, from right to right, till she
The woman-phantom, she that seemed no more
Than the man's shadow in a glass.

Canto VI., Line 316.

Rang ruin, answered full of grief and scorn.
What! in our time of glory when the cause
Now stands up, first, a trophied pillar—now
So clipt, so stinted in our triumph—barred
Ev'n from our free heart-thanks, and every way
Thwarted and vext, and lastly catechised
By our own creature! one that made our laws!
Our great she-Solon! her that built the nest
To hatch the cuckoo! whom we called our friend!
But we will crush the lie that glances at us
As cloaking in the larger charities
Some baby predilection; all amazed!
We must amaze this legislator more.
Fling our doors wide!

Line 325.

But shall not. Pass and mingle with your likes
Go, help the half-brained dwarf Society,
To find low motives unto noble deeds,
To fix all doubt upon the darker side;

> *Go, fitter there for narrowest neighbourhoods,*
> *Old talker, haunt where gossip breeds and seethes.*
> *And festers in provincial sloth! and you,*
> *That think we sought to practise on a life*
> *Risk'd for our own and trusted to our hands,*
> *What say you, Sir? you hear us; deem ye not*
> *'Tis all too like that even now we scheme,*
> *In one broad death confounding friend and foe,*
> *To drug them all? revolve it: you are man,*
> *And therefore no doubt wise; but after this*
> We brook no further insult, but are gone.

These two last omissions are the only important ones. They occur in the Princess Ida's speech before she opens her college as an hospital for the wounded knights. The character of Ida gains by the omission, for it did not become her to enter into a scolding match with such a mistress of tongue-fence as Lady Blanche.

The Epilogue has been much altered. All the matter relating to the French Revolution was inserted. The Poet's mind was no doubt full of the turmoil in France which broke out shortly after the publication of the first edition, but the poem is not improved as a work of art by the insertion of what must be called extraneous matter. Some lines omitted at the very beginning throw a little light on the plan of the poem.

> *Here closed our compound story, which at first*
> *Had only meant to banter little maids*
> *With mock heroics and with parody:*
> *But slipt in some strange way, crost with burlesque,*
> *From mock to earnest, even into tones*
> *Of tragic and with less and less of jest*
> *To such a serious end.*

The Epilogue is, however, in reality re-written and expanded so much as to be practically new work. The Prologue, also, is largely expanded. The Interlude is entirely new, but omissions seldom occur in the poem ; the changes made are substitutions of words, insertions of lines, or of passages to bring out the meaning, and innumerable minute touches to impart finish to the style and rhythm to the verse.

THE VERSIFICATION OF "THE PRINCESS."

Professor Hadley's essay upon this poem contains some remarks upon its versification which are not only excellent of themselves, but valuable as stimulating to further study in the same direction. He says :—

"Mr. Tennyson has evidently taken extraordinary pains with the construction of his verse. He seems to have felt that a single measure running through a long poem must of necessity become monotonous and wearisome, unless great care can be taken to diversify its rhythm. . . . . Certain it is that in affluence of means and in variety of effects, the blank verse of *The Princess* surpasses all its author's previous attempts in the same kind of measure ; nor would it be easy to find its equal in these respects since the time of Milton. To the versification of the *Paradise Lost*, the greatest exemplar of versification in the English language, Mr. Tennyson, it is clear, has given no little attention ; and from this poem, and from the older English poetry in general, he has adopted many rhythmical and metrical expedients—liberties or licenses, as they are sometimes called—which the too finical taste of later times, and the undue passion for uniformity, have generally discarded. Among these we mention the so-called elision—more truly, the blending of a final vowel with the vowel initial of a following word into a single syllable, or at least what passes for such in the rhythm. Thus we have—

> That made *the old* warrior from his ivied nook
> Glow like a sunbeam.

The violet varies from *the lily* as far
As oak from elm.

O Swallow, *Swallow, if* I could *follow and* light
Upon her lattice.

So, too, where the second word begins with a weak consonant easily elided in pronunciation :—

Fly *to her*, and pipe and *woo her*, and make her mine.

You must not *slay him;* he risked his life for ours.

The same fusion occurs often in a single word, and not only in such forms as *lovelier, sapience,* &c., where all our poets have employed it, but in many instances where the last two centuries have renounced its use. Thus in the following lines the words *seeing, crying, highest,* go for monosyllables in the rhythm :—

And Cyril *seeing* it, pushed against the prince.

Some *crying* there was an army in the land.

And *highest* among the statues, statue-like.

The combinations *in the, of the,* &c., are often treated as filling but one rhythmical place—

Better have died, and spilt our bones *in the* flood.

Poets, whose thoughts enrich the blood *of the* world.

When the man wants weight, the woman takes it up.

In many instances a short syllable is neglected—that is, does not count as forming by itself a place in the metre. In the following quotation, the words *enemy, general, soluble,* are treated as dissyllables—

Now she lightens scorn
At *the enemy* of her plan, but then would hate
The *general* foe. More *soluble* is the knot.

Especially does this occur when a short final syllable is followed by a word beginning with a vowel—

H

A *palace* in our own land, where you shall reign.

A tent of *satin* elaborately wrought.

We could distinguish other cases, in which a reader unfamiliar with the earlier English rhythms might be offended by supernumerary syllables; but to enter upon long details would perhaps be more tedious than profitable. In none of these instances, if we may judge of Mr. Tennyson's pronunciation from his way of writing, would he omit a syllable in reading; nor does the rhythm of the verse (let metrical doctors, like Mr. Guest, say what they please about it) require of us the use of any such expedient."

Many passages also occur of irregular rhythm in which, as in the *Paradise Lost*, the sound is suited to the sense to a degree not excelled by Milton or Virgil. Such are—

> Palpitated, her hand shook, and we heard
> In the dead hush the papers that she held
> Rustle;

> And in the blast and bray of the long horn
> And serpent-throated bugle, undulated
> The banner;

> The dark, when clocks
> Throbbed thunder thro' the palace floors.

> Brake with a blast of trumpets from the gate.

> While the great organ almost burst his pipes,
> Groaning for power, and rolling thro' the courts
> A long melodious thunder to the sound
> Of solemn psalms, and silver litanies.

> And up we came to where the river sloped
> To plunge in cataract, shattering on black blocks
> A breadth of thunder. O'er it shook the woods,
> And danced the colour.

> And the flood drew, yet I caught her, then
> Oaring one arm, and bearing in my left
> The weight of all the hopes of half the world,
> Strove to buffet to land in vain.
>
> Myriads of rivulets hurrying through the lawn,
> The moan of doves in immemorial elms,
> And murmuring of innumerable bees.

'Who,' asks Kingsley, 'after three such lines, will talk of English as a harsh and clumsy language, and seek in the effeminate and monotonous Italian for expressive melody of sound? Who cannot hear in them the rapid rippling of the water, the stately calmness of the wood-dove's note, and in the repetition of short syllables and soft liquids in the last line, the

> murmuring of innumerable bees?'

It will be observed at once, on reading these and similar passages aloud, that much of their power depends upon alliteration. This, which in the old Saxon poetry stood for modern rhyme, adds a charming variety to the versification of *The Princess*. It abounds throughout all Tennyson's writings, for his mind is steeped in the older literature of England, but especially in this poem, *e.g.*—

> With prudes for proctors, dowagers for deans,
> And sweet girl-graduates in their golden hair.

> And died
> Of fright in far apartments.

Sweet thoughts would swarm, as bees about their queen.

> The lark
> Shot up and shrilled in flickering gyres.

It is useless to multiply instances. They pervade the whole poem."

TENNYSON AS A WORD-PAINTER.

Philip Hamerton, in his *Thoughts about Art*, has written well upon the advantages and limitations of word-painting compared with colour-painting. He places the best modern word-painters in verse in the following order of excellence: Tennyson, Shelley, Byron, Scott, Wordsworth, and Keats. Tennyson he places first, and he quotes Ruskin as saying that no description of his is worth four lines of Tennyson. He shows that word description is infinitely limited in its power over form and colour as compared with the pictorial art, and he thinks that Tennyson understands these limits better than any other modern poet, and therefore never becomes tedious by straining after fidelities unattainable by verbal art. That is no doubt true, but the poet is compensated for these limitations by the superior power he possesses of expressing sound and motion. Many passages occur in *The Princess*, in which both kinds of descriptive power are shown; for instance—

> All about his motion clung
> The shadow of his sister, as the beam
> Of the east, that play'd upon them, made them glance
> Like those three stars of the airy giant's zone,
> That glitter burnished by the frosty dark;
> And as the fiery Sirius alters hue,
> And bickers into red and emerald, shone
> Their morions, washed with morning as they came.

> Fixt like a beacon-tower above the waves
> Of tempest, when the crimson rolling eye
> Glares ruin, and the wild birds on the light
> Dash themselves dead.

> And spill
> Their thousand wreaths of dangling water smoke,
> That like a broken purpose waste in air.

> And then to bed, where half in doze I seemed
> To float about a glimmering night, and watch
> A full sea glazed with muffled moonlight, swell
> On some dark shore just seen that it was rich.

> Reels as the golden autumn woodland reels
> Athwart the smoke of burning leaves.

> Morn in the white wake of the morning star
> Came furrowing all the Orient into gold.

Compare the sunset—

>   Till the Sun
> Grew broader toward his death, and fell, and all
> The rosy heights came out above the lawns,
> And she, as one that climbs a peak to gaze
> O'er land and main, and sees a great black cloud
> Drag inward from the deeps, a wall of night,
> Blot out the slope of sea from verge to shore,
> And suck the blinding splendour from the sand,
> And quenching lake by lake, and tarn by tarn,
> Expunge the world !

The poem contains many such pictorial descriptions, which, if excelled by painting in preciseness of colour, are full of movement unattainable upon canvas. It is impossible to resist giving a few more descriptive passages.

> Sees the midsummer midnight, Norway sun
> Set into sunrise.

Woman's love unworthily bestowed is vividly described—

>   Their sinless faith
> A maiden moon that sparkles on a sty,
> Glorifying clown and satyr.

The three friends early on the first morning in the college—

　　　　　　　　　　　　　　High
Above the empurpled champaign, drank the gale
That, blown about the foliage underneath,
And sated with the innumerable rose,
Beat balm upon our eyelids.

THE POET AS INTERPRETER OF THE AGE.

The following extract from F. W. Robertson is perhaps the most justly appreciative criticism of Tennyson which has ever appeared. It is from a lecture upon English poetry, delivered to the working-men of Brighton in 1852:—

"I ranked Tennyson in the first order, because with great mastery over his material—words, great plastic power of versification and a rare gift of harmony, he has also vision or insight ; and because feeling intensely the great questions of the day, not as a mere man of letters, but as a man, he is to some extent the interpreter of his age, not only in its mysticism, which I tried to show you is the necessary reaction from the rigid formulas of science and the earthliness of an age of work, into the vagueness which belongs to infinitude, but also in his poetic and almost prophetic solution of some of its great questions.

"Thus in his *Princess*, which he calls a 'medley,' the former half of which is sportive, and the plot almost too fantastic and impossible for criticism, while the latter portion seems too serious for a story so light and flimsy, he has with exquisite taste disposed of the question which has its burlesque and comic as well as its tragic side, of woman's present place and future destinies. And if any one wishes to see this subject treated with a masterly and delicate hand, in protest alike against the theories which would make her as the man, which she could only be by becoming masculine, not manly, and those which would have her to remain the toy, or the slave, or the slight thing of sentimental and frivolous accomplishment which education has hitherto aimed at making her, I would recommend him to study the few last pages of *The Princess*, where the poet brings the question back, as a poet should, to nature; develops the ideal out of the actual woman, and reads out of what she is, on the one hand, what her Creator intended her to be, and on the other, what she never can or ought to be."—*Rev. F. W. Robertson, Lectures and Addresses.*

BIBLIOGRAPHY OF "THE PRINCESS."

It seems appropriate to close this study with a list of the various editions of the poem, and the present prices in the London booksellers' shops.

First Edition, pp. 164; published 1847.

Priced in original cloth binding, £1, 15s.

Second Edition, pp. 164; published 1848.

The dedication to Henry Lushington was added to this edition, and a few verbal changes made. Priced cloth, uncut, 16s.

Third Edition, pp. 177; published 1850.

This edition was thoroughly revised. Large additions were made in the body of the poem. The songs and the interlude were added, and the poet's thought fully expressed. Priced in original cloth, 7s. 6d.

Fourth Edition, pp. 182; published 1851.

In this, all the passages about the weird seizures of the Prince were inserted. The fourth song was altered to what it now is. The second stanza of the first song was omitted, but restored in subsequent editions. Priced 7s. 6d.

Fifth Edition, pp. 183; published 1853.

> In this, the passage in the Prologue commencing "O miracle of woman," and ending—"So sang the gallant glorious chronicle," was first inserted. In this edition the text was settled as we now have it.

In America *The Princess* was published by Ticknor & Fields, of Boston, in 1848. It was reprinted from the first edition of 1847. In 1855 the same publishers issued a collected edition of Tennyson's works, containing this poem reprinted from the fifth edition. At the present time the first edition can be bought in Boston for 3*s.* sterling.

THE END.

A STUDY OF "THE PRINCESS."

BY S. E. DAWSON.

NOTICES OF THE PRESS.

LONDON SATURDAY REVIEW.—It is sensible, simple, and to the point. To us, who almost know the poem by heart, it has served to illustrate some imperfectly comprehended allusions, to throw some light on imperfectly appreciated beauties; and, if we cannot wholly agree with the writer's views, we can recommend the " Study " to ordinary readers of Tennyson as well worthy the slight demand which its perusal will make upon their leisure.

LONDON ACADEMY.—It is careful, not often trivial, sometimes acute, and generally appreciative of what Mr. Dawson is quite right in regarding as, on the whole, the least justly appreciated of all the Laureate's larger works.

LIVERPOOL MERCURY.—This is a thoughtful and charming little monograph upon one of the most thoughtful and charming of Tennyson's poems. Mr. Dawson has done his work exceedingly well. Even those who are most familiar with the poem on which it treats, cannot rise from a perusal of this explanation and commentary, without possessing new lights and a better understanding of the poet's meaning and intention.

NEW YORK CRITIC.—Mr. Dawson's argument and analysis of the poem, while it is ingenious and shows a good deal of study as well as much cleverness and aptness in criticism, will hardly compass his purpose. It is the pleasing work of an enthusiast, who finds in Tennyson what is not there.

HARPERS' MAGAZINE.—The mutations of opinion that have prevailed concerning the poem are ably summed up by Mr. S. E. Dawson, of Montreal, in a tasteful monograph entitled. " A Study, with critical and explanatory notes, of Alfred Tennyson's poem " The Princess," as a prelude to an exhaustive examination of the poem in its parts and as a whole. * * * Mr. Dawson is not a mere eulogist. While his graceful and delicate criticism is heartily appreciative, it is always keenly discriminating; and the criteria upon which he relies to show that as a work of art, "The Princess" is the most satisfying of all Tennyson's works, are as convincing as they are ingeniously and intelligently marshalled.

NEW YORK WORLD.—Written with the greatest appreciation and shows the author to be one of a growing number of admirers and students of Tennyson who place this poem in the foremost rank of the Laureate's work.

LONDON GRAPHIC.—A thoughtful and appreciative essay.

MANCHESTER (ENGLAND) CITY NEWS.—Mr. Dawson's little book is welcome on its own account, and he has done good service in writing his careful and pleasant critical estimate.

EDUCATIONAL MONTHLY.—Mr. Dawson writes both in an appreciative tone and with a thoroughness of insight which shows that he possesses one of the rarest of critical gifts, the power of estimating high-class poetry at its true value. We recommend his monograph on "The Princess" to all teachers as a most useful aid to the study of modern poetry.

THE CONTINENT (PHILADELPHIA).—That Tennyson requires any special expounding or critical analysis would at first sight seem impossible, but whoever takes up Mr. S. E. Dawson's little book "A Study, with critical and explanatory notes of Alfred Tennyson's poem, The Princess," will be surprised to discover what valuable aid these carefully prepared notes afford. Mr. Dawson gives the full history of the various changes in the poem made by the author, and an analysis of its plan and drift, which will be of value to every reader.

BOSTON TRAVELLER.—It is an excellent piece of work, appreciative without adulation, and critical without carping, of what is perhaps the masterpiece of the greatest poetical interpreter of this era.

NEW YORK DAILY GRAPHIC.—His argument is presented so clearly and ably as to command assent at once. * * * In pointing out in this concise manner what the central purpose of "The Princess" is, Mr. Dawson has performed a work that cannot be praised too highly.

WORCESTER (MASS) SPY.—Probably there is no other person who has studied "The Princess" so faithfully as Mr. Dawson has, and he has found it worthy of his study. He adds to his criticism a large number of curious and valuable notes, some of them merely explanatory, some historical, but most of them literary, giving the passages in other authors similar to those in the Princess, and the parallel passages in Tennyson's other poems. * * * Every lover of Tennyson will find real pleasure in Mr. Dawson's analysis, criticism and praise of the poem, whether he agrees with him or not.

NOTICES OF THE PRESS.

LITERARY REVIEW (BOSTON).—This volume cannot but be welcome to all Tennysonians.

BOSTON DAILY ADVERTISER.—It is a positive pleasure to read so deliberate a criticism of a purely literary kind. It gives one a sense of leisure and serenity in pleasant intellectual work, and renews something of the delight that Tennyson's poems gave us thirty years ago.

THE DETROIT FREE PRESS.—An acute and exhaustive analysis. · · · He certainly presents the poem in many new and attractive aspects and throws new light upon many passages which have hitherto been much misapprehended.

EDINBURGH SCOTSMAN.—A very thoughtful and sympathetic estimate of a poem which we agree with him in thinking "singularly under-rated." · · · Mr. Dawson displays a thorough grasp of the poet's intention, and is able to discern the underlying unity and consistency of design and purpose which the poem really possesses. People who read "The Princess" after going through this book will find themselves better qualified to understand it, and to do justice to the genius of its author.

WESTERN TIMES, (BRISTOL, ENGLAND).—The author appears to have the true inspiration for his work, and will be sure of the greatest thanks of all who appreciate the Laureate—so notable for his tenderness, insight into moral truth, and lyric beauty.

ST. JOHN, N. B., TELEGRAPH.—Mr. Dawson's essay is graceful, polished and firm; his manner is dignified and urbane, discreetly disguising such occasional covert laughter as might well be provoked by some of his more blundering antagonists.

KNOX COLLEGE (TORONTO) MONTHLY.—The best defender of "The Princess" we have met.

TORONTO MAIL.—A dainty little volume, on a very pleasing topic and written with a skill and fineness of appreciation which are very noticeable.

CINCINNATI COMMERCIAL.—This is a refreshing criticism, and an instructive array of notes.

CANADIAN ILLUSTRATED NEWS.—Students of Tennyson owe a debt of gratitude to Mr. Dawson for his charming little volume.

QUEBEC CHRONICLE.—Perfect as a piece of criticism, sympathetic in the main and always bright and scholarly.

MONTREAL GAZETTE.—The "Notes" display the loving care, thought and research to which the "Study" throughout abundantly testifies.

www.ingramcontent.com/pod-product-compliance
Lightning Source LLC
Chambersburg PA
CBHW020100170426
43199CB00009B/347